MUSINGS
from MAIN STREET

Robert H. Linders

Musings from Main Street

iUniverse books may be ordered through booksellers or by contacting:

iUniverse
1663 Liberty Drive
Bloomington, IN 47403
www.iuniverse.com
844-349-9409

ISBN: 978-1-6632-3882-5 (sc)
ISBN: 978-1-6632-3844-3 (e)

Library of Congress Control Number: 2022907556

Print information available on the last page.

iUniverse rev. date: 05/26/2022

CONTENTS

WHERE THE GARDEN GROWS

Do you remember the band, REM? One of their old songs has been rising these past few weeks and for good reason. Remember the lyrics? "It's the end of the world as we know it, and I feel fine." The Pointer Sisters' lyrics also hauntingly coming to life: "I'm about to lose control and I think I like it… " How so? Well, think about your life a few weeks ago: rushing here, rushing there, wondering what happened to the week just past! A friend sent me a poster reading: "I'm not bored but did you know I had two bags of rice in the pantry and one had 2411 grains in it and the other only 2355 grains"?

Last week florists in Philadelphia—their shops forced to close—made their way to Rittenhouse Square and turned the square into a munificent garden of delight—a feast for the eyes. Emily Dickinson would be pleased! And so would Wordsworth! Check out the poems below. They made me think of a verse from John's passion—so fitting for Lent: "At the place where he was crucified there was a garden." May it be so for us!

If I can stop one Heart from breaking, by Emily Dickinson
If I can stop one Heart from breaking,
I shall not live in vain
If I can ease one Life the Aching,
Or cool one Pain,

Or help one fainting Robin
Unto his Nest again,
I shall not live in vain.
Excerpt from *Tintern Abbey*, by William Wordsworth
On that best portion of a good man's life,
His little, nameless, unremembered, acts
Of kindness and of love.

FROM MY ISOLATION ROOM

Last Sunday afternoon my land line phone rang. I was utterly surprised and ecstatic to hear this message: "Bob, how about another boiled ham dinner?" Herschel is 97. He has for decades been the largest potato farmer in Aroostook County, Maine.

Back in the 1980s—after my father died—I flew to Presque Isle to meet Herschel for the first time. I drove with him to his camp deep in the North Woods (30 miles from the nearest road!) to hunt ruffed grouse. One large bird, which I named Roger, sits proudly in my office. I shot Roger with my grandfather's Parker 12 gauge shotgun. This rifle is now housed in an elegant gun case, crafted out of a fine piece of cherry, by our own Bruce Burkhart.

Memories—how they come surging back into the human heart to accuse or to make clean. Herschel—quarantined at home with his wife, Betty—was perusing old photos. He spotted one of me eating a boiled ham dinner deep in the North Woods of Maine. He thought of me and my father and my father's father. I wonder: as we sit sheltered in our homes awaiting a word of hope, is there someone we can call? There is a story in the Bible (Luke 5) of a man in great need. Jesus saw him and we read: "Jesus reached out his hand and touched him." In these difficult days, I believe our Lord calls us to do as much!

SHOES

The Bible doesn't say much about shoes. My RSV concordance lists only nine such references in the entire Bible. Perhaps the most significant reference appears in Luke 15—Jesus, parable of the Prodigal Son. We read that when the prodigal returned, his father was so overjoyed to receive his wayward son that he ordered: "Quick! Fetch a robe, the best we have, and put it on him; put a ring on his finger and shoes on his feet."

Several years ago, when my daughter was in the 8th grade at a track meet, I watched a young girl from Truman Middle School win the 200 meter race wearing a much worn pair of sneakers—not meant for running. I contacted Truman and offered to buy her a pair of sneakers and even coach her. Sadly, the school was not able to put me in touch with the young girl in light of so many cases of children being exploited by adults in positions of authority.

Those who have studied slavery in our country know well how many spirituals make reference to shoes. Paul Robeson sings: "All God's children got shoes—when I get to heaven going to put on my shoes and going to walk all over God's heaven." Of course, our best modern prophets were quick to remind us that we also need shoes here on earth and that at its best love cannot be separated from justice!

Early this morning my wife introduced me to "Marketplace," which I now know is on my seldom-used Facebook.. We drove to a simple duplex home in Hatfield. A bag was hanging on the door with my wife's name attached. She took the bag and placed the requested six dollars under door mat. When we got home, my wife showed me eight pairs of never-worn baby shoes. I googled a few of the brands and soon realized the shoes were worth over $200! Needless to say, "Marketplace" has a new convert!

The great paradox of this plague, of course, is that we had to be set apart in order to feel together. I never would have guessed a few weeks ago that riding to Hatfield to get a bargain on eight pairs of baby shoes by recycling would be the big event of the day! Truth be told, there is no joy for any until there is joy for all. We are all in this together. Rugged individualism needs to be wed to a sense of community.

In the biblical view, when we are separated from community, like Cain in his banishment, we suffer loneliness and misery. We were never meant to freelance our experience of God. St. Paul says: *"How beautiful are the feet of those who bring good news."* This lovely text implies God's blessing both on those who give and those who receive. I have visions of our new granddaughter, Hadley, wearing those shoes, and in time our sharing with her photos of her wearing them and also sharing with her how in the midst of the "Plague of 2020" our driving to Hatfield to buy them for her. In our basement is a bag with my dad's leather track shoes, which he wore running against Jesse Owens in the 1930s. I recall in the 10th grade stuffing cotton in those shoes, because they were too big for me, as I made a decision to become a runner too.

The prophet Ezekiel wrote in 586 B.C. Jerusalem was under siege. It was a time of great distress. Yet Ezekiel spoke of resurrection and new life. He wrote: *"Do not complain. Wrap your turban on your head, put on your shoes and eat not the bread of sorrow."* Amen!

EMMA

A few weeks ago, before the onset of Covid-19, I started my walk into town to see the new film, *Emma*, playing at the County Theatre. I didn't get far when a neighbor said, "The theatre is closed until further notice." A good move to be sure. All our best scientists tell us that "physical distancing" is the best weapon we have against this virus.

As an alternative, back home I began reading *Emma*. One night, Pastor Rusert and I spent an enjoyable three hours discussing this classic novel with his wonderful English professor at the College of New Jersey. Early on in the book I was struck by this sentence: *"I should like to see Emma in love, and in some doubt of a return. It would do her good."* A quintessential Jane Austen sentence to be sure! Emma is beautiful, high-spirited, intelligent, wealthy and spoiled.

A professor of music once quipped of a talented young singer, "She will be great some day when someone breaks her heart." Adversity can take us into the deep. When a parent loses a child, the last thing I want to say is, "I know how you feel." The first thing I want to say is, "I am so sorry for your loss. When you are ready, I would like to introduce you to someone who recently went through what you are going through now."

As Thornton Wilder put it, *"In the Lord's army only the wounded can serve."* There is a passage in the Book of Hebrews that has stuck with me over the years: *"He learned obedience in the school of suffering."* This is not a school we wish to attend—even on a full scholarship! Yet, truth be told, if we are to "go deep," it's a school we cannot avoid. But, of course, we seldom have a choice. The pandemic of the past few weeks is the only example we need.

I have watched, as you have, doctors, nurses, respiratory therapists, aides, grocery store clerks and others put their lives on the line. On the news this morning I vividly witnessed a young man whose job is disinfecting hospital rooms after someone has died or been moved. He does this day after day. He feels it is his calling. It is his "school of suffering" and he knows he will never be the same.

Whether his experience will make him bitter or better depends on many variables—not the least of which is his response to the gratuitous evil he is facing every day. An image of God that makes sense to me is that of "Divine Alchemist." I believe God is able to transmute evil into good. We recall every Holy Week that Pilate had Jesus crucified and put a period after the deed, but God changed the period to a comma for the story was to be continued. Such is the heart of our faith. Yes, there is much randomness and evil in this unfinished world—a world that has rightly been called "the 8th day of creation." But we live in hope that God isn't finished with us and in time will turn us into what we were meant to be.

Emma is off to an inauspicious beginning, but Jane Austen wisely knows that some unexpected rejection will confront her soon enough and test her mettle. A modern poet put it well:

I took a walk with pleasure she chattered all the way
And left me none the wiser for all she had to say.
I took a walk with sorrow and ne'er a word said she
But oh the things I learned from her when sorrow walked with me.

VIRUS, VALUE AND VANITY

A few weeks ago columnist Phil Gianficaro wrote an amusing piece in *The Intelligencer* about the closing of hair salons and the consequences this will have in coming weeks as the real blondes (and brunettes?) are separated from the not-so-real. Phil's column has me thinking about Samson. Biblical scholars are in agreement that Samson's tragic demise portrays what happens when a person with charisma disregards the guidance of the Lord in a time of crisis to pursue personal ambitions.

A timely tale: Samson allows Delilah to seduce and then deceive him. His hair is inseparable from his strength in the story and once his hair is cut he becomes weak and helpless.

"All is vanity," says the Hebrew Bible. Ah, but how slow we are to learn. There is a prophetic line in Shakespeare's *King Lear* where the loyal Kent turns to the shallow Oswald and says: "A tailor made thee." Yes, we can spend much time on hair stylists and the expensive products they sell us, but it matters little if at the end of the day someone can say of us: "A barber made thee..."

The passion narratives remind us that Jesus died with one possession: a seamless tunic for which four soldiers gambled at the foot of the cross. He died in weakness but in that weakness was his strength. In losing he wins. In dying he reigns. In giving away his life, he reveals a love that never quits and never lets us go. Such is the shape of Holy Week. Clothing, hair, shoes count for little and will not save us from this invisible virus surrounding us nor will they give meaning to our daily existence.

So, yes, let's approve federal aid to our barbers and hair salons just as we would for any honest small business. Caring for our hair is a noble vocation and heaven only knows how much sage advice these barbers and hair stylists give to us their loyal clients, as we come to them every few weeks (until recently!) looking for affirmation and a better coiffure.

Fair enough, but remember, as our mission statement says: "Our worth is a divine gift not a human achievement." Our value comes from a God who, Jesus says, has "counted even the hairs of your head."

In my ministry I've officiated at over 800 funerals and not once have I ever had a U-Haul follow us to the cemetery. When we die we leave behind everything we have and take with us everything we are. What we hope to leave behind is what the poet Wordsworth called "our little unremembered acts of kindness and love." What a tribute if we live so nobly that when we die people will say of us what Yeats said of Robert Gregory: "What made us dream that he could comb grey hair?"

Hear these words of Shakespeare to the dead Percy in *Henry IV*: "Farewell, brave Soul. Ill- weaved ambition, how much art thou shrunk! When that this body did contain a spirit, a kingdom for it was too small a bound. But now two paces of the vilest earth is room enough."

Or, as Jesus put it: "Do not store up for yourselves treasure on earth, where moth and rust destroy and thieves break in and steal; for where your treasure is, there will your heart be also."

A YELLOW SACRAMENT

Have you noticed the many blooming forsythias these past few days? I'm sure you have taken delight in these yellow sacraments of spring--along with the tall, upright tulips, intricate daffodils and always welcome cherry blossoms--beckoning us to behold beauty in the midst of our sadness. This has been especially true for me. A dear friend, Bob Bauers, died a few weeks ago. He was in his late 90s with a mind as sharp as they come. Reading via his Kindle, he was forever urging me to read whatever moved him and inspired his curiosity.

Bob was a stickler for grammar, pronunciation and just about anything else that struck his fancy. One topic on which we differed was the pronunciation of "forsythia." Bob insisted on pronouncing the word with a long "I" after the Scottish botanist, William Forsyth (1737—1804). I told Bob that if ever I uttered such silliness from the pulpit, parishioners and visitors alike would not pay attention to me for the next ten minutes! Such "dilettante" behavior, I told him, would be a petty, a foolish distraction! I reminded him that language changes over time and so does pronunciation. I never persuaded him even though I still think I was right!

However, now that he has left us, I cannot utter the word "forsythia" without saying, "Bob said we must pronounce it with a long "I" in honor of William Forsyth!" How strange is life and death! Edward Garrigan died last week. He was rector of St. Paul's Episcopal Church here in town for 25 years. He was a good friend. I was best man at his wedding. Yesterday John Vannorsdall died. He was my chaplain at college and then went on to succeed the legendary William Sloan Coffin as chaplain of Yale University.

When first I heard John preach, I was not impressed. He kept using words like "ambiguity," "ambivalence", "mixed motives." I was young and foolish and wanted more clarity and fewer nuances! Needless to say, he won me over. He taught me, in the words of one of his famous sermons, "to leave simpleness and live and walk in the way of insight." Perhaps of all the preachers whose style and content I've shared with Pastor Rusert, the one who has perhaps influenced him the most has been John Vannorsdall.

I have often called those whom we have loved and lost our "balcony people"—those dear souls who are now part of the company of heaven and cheer us on as we run our earthly race, winding our way through this world in search of our true home, the "land of the great King." Each year prior to their First Communion, I like to tell our 5th graders that a sacrament is a thing of molecules to remind us of things not made of molecules: water, bread and wine. Expanding on this definition, the Scottish theologian, Donald Ballie, has invited us to consider that we live in a sacramental universe. If this be so, then even "forsythias" can be called sacraments—pointing us to God who is our true home.

WHEN BAD THINGS HAPPEN

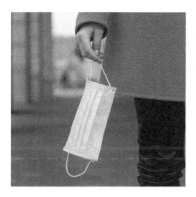

"Only 700 died today—Thank God! Thank God! Thank God!" These words made the front page of today's *the New York Times*. I don't believe those who say such things mean any harm. Yet I hear God's name used in such a casual way and I wonder, "What does such talk mean?" Is it just harmless chatter, a pious platitude? Do those who say such things believe God took only 700 lives today when He might have chosen to take 900?

When I teach the Second Commandment to our 8th graders, I ask them to consider a costly piece of Waterford crystal handed down to their parents from their great grandparents. Surely such a treasure is to be afforded greater respect than say a mere glass mug purchased at Dollar Tree for one dollar. I believe it is the same with words. It is fitting to treat words about holy and sacred things with great respect. It seems inappropriate, as the Second Commandment behooves us, to use sacred words loosely—"in vain." The 8th graders get it. Even if they are not comfortable confronting those who curse, I hope they at least will refrain from doing so.

Going a bit deeper, I would ask: what does it mean to say, "Only 700 people died today, thank God!" The French mystic, Simone Weil, wrote: "God ceases to be everything so we can be something." It seems to me many terrible things happen in this world which are not God's will or intention. We humans abuse our freedom and hurt each other and then as Jesus said, "the rain shines on the evil and on the good." One skeptic quipped after a hurricane struck his city: "Why did the hurricane destroy the church and spare the brothel?"

Thornton Wilder reminded us in one of his plays that we live "in the 8th day of creation." The world is unfinished. God is working still. The theologian, John A.T. Robinson, struggling with cancer, wrote that God was "in the cancer." He did not mean God sent the cancer but that God was with him in his suffering working to bring something of value out of this dreaded disease. I like the image of God as an Ingenious Alchemist who is forever working with us to transmute the lead of evil into the gold of growth and blessing.

My favorite definition of Providence comes from the theologian, Paul Tillich: "Providence does not mean a divine, efficient machine. Rather providence means that there is a creative and saving possibility implied in every situation, which cannot be destroyed by any event."

We see such signs of divine providence all around us--people who become not bitter but better by the creative way they respond to the randomness of life. G.K. Chesterton said, "Jesus was crucified on a stick but somehow managed to get hold of the right end of it." This is our Easter hope. It means despair is presumptuous. The symbol of our faith is an instrument of death. This suggests at the very least, hope.

THE CRUELEST MONTH

In 1922, in his poem, *The Waste Land*, T.S. Eliot called April the cruellest month. The poem reads:

April is the cruelest month, breeding
Lilacs out of the dead land, mixing
Memory and desire, stirring
Dull roots with spring rain.
Winter kept us warm, covering
Earth in forgetful snow, feeding
A little life with dried tubers.

I think I know what he means. I've conducted funerals in the spring. It's hard to lose someone, drive home, see all nature singing with new life—and be unable to join the chorus. I suspect April is the cruelest month because the life and color of spring forces painful memories to surface.

Emily Dickinson wrote that after a great pain "a formal feeling comes." We feel vulnerable, and even if we believe in our heads "vulnerability is the birthplace of courage," it is hard to take that longest of all journeys- the journey from head to heart.

Back in 1939, C.S. Lewis delivered a sermon in Oxford titled, "Learning in War-Time." He said: "The war creates no absolutely new situation.....Human life has always been lived on the precipice. We are mistaken if we compare war with 'normal life.' Life has never been normal. Even those periods we think most tranquil turn out, on closer inspection, to be full of cries, alarms, difficulties, emergencies."

Lewis certainly puts things in perspective, and he did so before many of us were even born! The question before us, of course, is how we choose to respond. In 1758, Voltaire wrote his classic novel, *Candide*. The young Candide gets off to a good start in life and then everything falls apart for him—every conceivable misfortune, tragedy, and form of abuse. In the end of the tale, Volataire suggests how we can crush the horror. He says simply, "We need to work our fields." Some render the French: "Make our gardens grow."

I love those ancient words of the prophet Isaiah: "Those who wait on the Lord will renew their strength, they will mount up with wings like eagles, they shall run and not be weary, and they shall walk and not faint."

I wonder: Did Isaiah get the progression backwards? Every new parent knows that first we crawl, then we walk, then we run! Ah, but on second thought, maybe Isaiah has gotten hold of a more profound truth. When the going gets tough, the real heroes are not those who "mount up with wings like eagles." The real heroes are those who "work their fields," "keep on keeping on," putting one foot in front of the other. Yet, we do so in sure and certain hope that the end of it all is not a whimpering into death, but God's triumphant yes. So, as I've said at so many Easters past: "Bloom, Frozen Christian, April stands before your door."

THE NEXT TIME

While working in the 1970s on a graduate degree in English, I had a young professor who introduced us to Isabel Archer. He believed Henry James' classic novel, *Portrait of a Lady*, was the greatest novel in our language. I was surprised to hear such words from our strikingly young professor, who drove each week from Vermont to New Jersey in an uncanny fancy little sports car and had two steamy novels on the *New York Times* best seller list! A Henry James classic, published in 1880, hardly seemed to befit his personality.

During today's confinement, I decided to get better acquainted with Isabel, the chief character in the novel. She is a formidable young woman: smart, rich, attractive, self-confident. Her cousin, Ralph, thinks Lord Warburton would be the perfect husband. Ralph, an astute observer, says to Isabel: "I don't think it's presumptuous of me to suggest you will gain more than you will lose marrying him."

Isabel refuses Lord Warburton. Ralph cannot understand and says to Isabel: "What's the logic? He has hardly a fault!" Isabel replies: "I don't wish to marry him. That's the logic." Pressed she says: "The world interests me and I want to throw myself into it." As the novel progresses, Isabel makes some tragic choices. Henry James brilliantly explores her motives and the consequences of the choices she makes.

I think it's fair to say we all make poor choices and live with the consequences. A modern poet, Mark Strand, put it this way in a poem titled, "The Next Time."

Perfection is out of the question for people like us...
It could have been another story,
The one that was meant instead of the one that happened.

Yes, there is always another story—the perfect story, the one that was meant to be. If only life were like a TV drama where we could push the pause button, rewind, rewrite the script and do it right this time! Life affords us no such luxury. Those virus infected animals in China—if only, if only! As Mark Strand reminds us, "It could have been another story." True, but all we have is "the next time."

Here is where my understanding of providence comes in. I do not believe God micromanages his creation. Thomas Aquinas was moving in the right direction when he said: "God cannot do anything contrary to his nature of letting-be." Love is self-restricting when it comes to power.

St. Paul is often quoted as saying in Romans that "all things work together for good," but this is a poor translation of the original Greek text. It's not true. The next time may not be better. There is nothing automatic here. Yet I cling to the possibility that the next time will be better and thus take comfort in what Paul actually wrote: "God cooperates in all things for good with those who love him."

In these difficult days of isolation and uncertainty, it is comforting to know we are not alone. Yes, Isabel Archer, like all of us, will make some bad choices, but her worst decisions need not be her last decisions. They can be her next to last decisions--Thanks be to God!

ISABEL'S FALL

It's Sunday morning. I'm at church. I am the only one here. This hasn't happened here in over 150 years. Even during the last Sunday blizzard, a handful of us rolled a piano into the narthex and worshipped.

Last week in my Musing's blog, I introduced you to Henry James' *Portrait of a Lady*. Isabel Archer, the heroine in the story, had much going for her. Sadly, she learns that even in daylight on a clear highway it is possible to take a wrong turn.

Isabel wants freedom. Lord Warburton was too safe a choice and she refuses his proposal. Instead she marries a "total loser," Gilbert Osmond. Isabel would launch his boat for him. In her defective imagination she assumes she can change him, but Osmond is not open to change. Osmond deliberately "puts the lights out one by one." Osmond is a "sterile dilettante, a serpent in a bank of flowers." Isabel has "not read him right." Isabel was "deluded but dismally consistent." She had married a "factitious theory."

How did it happen? Henry James' definitive biographer, Leon Edel, says egotism and power, not love, are the real subjects of the book. Isabel's egotism certainly has blinded her from reality. Her cousin, Ralph, warns her not to marry Osmond. She ignores his warning. I spoke in a recent sermon about the importance of imagination. A truck gets stuck under an overpass. The police, the truck driver and a little boy all see the same facts but the little boy sees what the others do not see and says to the driver: "Mister, let the air out of the tires!" We might say faith is a "grown up imagination." I called it an "interpretive style." Yes, just let the air out of the tires.

Fair enough! Yet one might also have a "defective imagination." Such was the case of Isabel Archer. We've been hearing much of late about "cognitive dissonance." You know smoking is bad for you but you do it anyway. The opposite of "cognitive dissonance" is "cognitive assonance."

Dr. Anthony Fauci, for me, is an example of the latter. He doesn't claim to have all the answers. Yet like any good scientist, he is always open to the coming of new light. Perhaps a few weeks ago he may have suggested putting a patient on a ventilator, but with the coming of new experience, he now employs "proning"—that is, turning patients on their sides and bellies with oxygen. In the words of the great hymn: "New occasions teach new duties." The historian Doris Kearns Goodwin speaks of how important it is that leaders surround themselves with a "team of rivals"—those willing to say, "The emperor has no clothes."

When we turn to the Bible, we see this truth in the witness of the prophets. Amos, Nathan, and John the Baptist come to mind. These brave souls were un-purchasable. They could not be bought. They were willing to speak "truth to power." One commentator said of Jesus: "He was not crucified for saying, 'Look at the lilies how they grow' but for saying, 'look at the thieves in the temple, how they steal.'"

Such truth, painful as it may be, sets us free. At the end of the novel, Isabel is on her knees at the bedside of her dying cousin, Ralph. She holds him in her arms and tells this brave truth teller that she is happier than she has been in a long time because in spite of everything, "love remains." Ah, if only it hadn't taken her so long!

DOG DAYS

Last week a member suggested I write a blog on dogs. I get it. In the past few weeks there have been more dogs on our streets than people. I've never seen so many dogs: big dogs, small dogs, short dogs, tall dogs, young dogs, old dogs. As we wear our masks and keep friends, neighbors and vulnerable loved ones six feet away, our dogs bring us comfort and consolation.

Yesterday on the morning news I learned dogs may help detect this new virus and thus protect us from exposure. I don't understand how this happens anymore than I understand how dogs can sniff cancer at our hospitals and drugs and terrorists at our airports. Yet I feel more secure when I arrive at an airport and see these wise four legged creatures! One of our members trains support dogs. One dog went on to help a young female college student in a wheelchair—actually handing the young lady's credit card to the cashier!

A friend shared with me a kind note he received from his vet after he put his dog down: "In their eyes we see a loving soul; in our hearts we know we will never have a finer friend." No wonder these loyal companions are all around us as we struggle to strike a balance between security and venturing out! Erich Fromm, the psychotherapist, once said every child needs a fatherly principle and a motherly principle. By a "fatherly principle," he meant the shaping power of expectation. We need someone near at hand to challenge us to strive for excellence and avoid mediocrity. Without such a demanding love, we will never achieve our potential.

However, too many expectations can wear us down! Thus we crave what Fromm called the "motherly principle." He meant unconditional love. This Jewish psychotherapist in his classic work, *The Art of Loving*, credited Luther for rediscovering the "motherly principle." In a word, grace! The poet, Robert Frost, put it this way: "Home is that place where when you go there they have to take you in."

Such unconditional love is the heart of our faith. It's why we say in our mission statement "our worth is a divine gift not a human achievement." Such unconditional love not only comforts us in our moments of grief and failure, but empowers us to face a new day with courage and self-confidence.

I love the way Lorraine Hansberry expressed this at the end of her play, *A Raisin in the Sun*. Mama says, "When do you think is the time to love somebody the most? When they done good and made things easy for everybody?...That ain't the time at all. It's when he's at his lowest and can't believe in hisself 'cause the world done whipped him so!"

Why so many dogs all around us as we face this pandemic? You know the answer! Perhaps my friend's vet said it best: "In their eyes we see a loving soul; in our hearts we know we will never have a finer friend."

One final theological postscript: If God's compassion is greater than ours, then how could God not love these creatures, great and small, as much as we do? I like these words St. Bonaventure penned in the 13th century: "Every creature by its very nature is a kind of effigy and likeness of the eternal wisdom."

RESTLESS

Today I want to explore with you a simple yet timely word: restless. The dictionary defines restless as being "without quiet or repose, never still or motionless." How difficult is this pandemic which has forced us to slow down! It's no doubt harder for those of us whose nature is such that we are always in motion!

I recall visiting a parishioner who suffered from "restless leg syndrome." He fell one night getting out of bed and spent weeks in physical rehabilitation. However you parse it, restless is not a pleasant word. I get restless on airplanes. Two hours is my limit. I've been considering a flight to California to visit my son and his wife. I asked my doctor if he had an Rx I might take. He responded, "Is it anxiety? Do you cling to the armrest?" Surprised, I replied, "No, I'm just full of energy." He suggested I drink a glass of wine to which I replied: "No, that won't do it. I need something stronger!" I did not tell him I titled my first book, "No Time for Rest," taken from a favorite hymn, "Come, Labor On."

In the 17th century one of our finest English poets, George Herbert, went about as deep as one can go with this word, restless. His poem, "The Pulley," imagines God pouring out with unsparing generosity his gifts of beauty and wisdom, honor and pleasure into the newly-made human heart. The poem then takes a twist. God holds back his gift of rest in fear that if God gave us all, we might adore the gifts instead of himself the giver. So, with fine insight Herbert has God say:

But keep them with repining restlessness;
Let him be rich and weary, that at least,
If goodness lead him not, yet weariness
May toss him to my breast.

George Herbert is a deeply religious poet. He believes there is a hunger that will not be put off forever—a yearning that will not forever be silent, a lust for reality that cannot be tamed by convention, a quest that cannot forever be led astray, a deep desire that will not always be content with husks. There is in all of us a great restlessness refusing to be deceived, refusing to be duped, refusing to be suppressed. It is the urge of the soul for completion. It is the quest of the soul for God.

In his poem the word "rest" has two senses: "remainder" and "repose." Herbert works them against one another. This seesaw suggests the pulley, which can draw us to God one way or the other. 1600 years before George Herbert, the writer of Luke's gospel shares with us Jesus' Parable of the Prodigal Son. In the parable, of course, both sons were restless and Luke seems to be saying, as does George Herbert, that one of two experiences will bring these two prodigals home to God: the misery of the far country or the lure of the Father's love.

300 years after Luke and 1300 years before George Herbert, St. Augustine summed it up in one memorable sentence: "Thou hast made us for thyself, O God, and our hearts are restless until they rest in thee."

THE LINDERS LIST: 2020 SUMMER READS

Reading much lately? Looking for some ideas? Several members suggested I devote a blog to summer reading. A good idea for sure, yet I feel a little like the proverbial mosquito in a nudist colony: Where shall I start with so much material? I started this list with books that have stirred my imagination and sparked me to go deeper. The list is surely subjective –perhaps to a fault. Hence I welcome discussing any of these with you!

Novels

Portrait of a Lady, Henry James
Madam Bovary, Gustav Flaubert
Saturday, Ian McEwan
Middlemarch, Geoge Eliot
Emma, Jane Austen

Biography

Hamilton, Ron Chernow
Washington, Ron Chernow
Samuel Johnson, W. Jackson Bate
John Adams, Douglas McCullough

Science and Religion

The New Cosmic Story, John Haught
Between Faith and Doubt, John Hick
The New Frontier of Religion and Science, John Hick

Grief

Tracks of a Fellow Struggler, John Claypool

Religious Reflection

The Devil and Dr. Church, F. Forrester Church
Entertaining Angels, F. Forrester Church
The Seven Deadly Virtues, F. Forrester Church
Letters to a Young Doubter, William Sloane Coffin
Credo, William Sloane Coffin
Wishful Thinking: A Seeker's ABC, Frederick Buechner
The Alphabet of Grace, Frederick Buechner
The Heart of Christianity, Marcus Borg
Meeting Jesus Again for the First Time, Marcus Borg
Evocations of Grace, Joseph Sittler
He Who Lets Us Be, Geddes MacGregor
Abba, John Cobb
Models of God, Sally McFague
The Good Book, Peter Gomes

Biblical Commentary

William Barclay
Poetry

Emily Dickinson
Mary Oliver

STRENGTH THROUGH RECOLLECTION

As my newest granddaughter grows by the hour, I've been thinking about memory and stumbled on this quote by American writer, William Maxwell: "I have liked remembering almost as much as I have liked living." It's been said we humans are only old when our memories are more precious than our hopes.

The poet Wordsworth, took this uniquely human experience to another level when he wrote:

Our birth is but a sleep and a forgetting...
Not in entire forgetfulness,
And not in utter nakedness,
But trailing clouds of glory do we come
From God, who is our home:
Heaven lies about us in our infancy!

We often lose our sense of wonder as we grow older. We've been here so often! We've done this so many times! There is so little in my life that is new! At a certain stage, the years go by more quickly --much like the second half of a roll of (rather scarce) toilet paper. The theologian, Reinhold Niebuhr, in a lovely essay, has suggested the secret of life is to recapture rather than retain the simplicities and profundities of childhood. Easier said than done---to be childlike, *not childish*!

Yesterday I reserved two seats at the (French) *Metro Bistrot* in Southbridge, Massachusetts. The chef is delightfully arrogant. He will not serve butter with his freshly baked homemade bread. He refuses to accommodate himself to your desires if those desires do not live up to his understanding of "fine dining." I love talking with him and my memory of past July experiences only heightens my anticipation of future encounters!

We humans live by memory and hope for what is the present, but memory tinged with anticipation? This is why I miss Holy Communion during this pandemic. The sacrament ties past, present and future together. We remember the night in which he was betrayed, we experience a presence in the here and now, and we anticipate a future consummation when "all the kingdoms of this world will be the kingdoms of our God and of his Christ."

There is an old Hebridean legend about a god who lives at the bottom of the sea. He could only live in the water but greatly desires a child. One day a child is being carried by boat from one island to another and the god tosses a wavelet into the child's heart. He says "The boy will come back to me for the sea is in his heart." I believe it. God hath set "eternity in our hearts."

I leave you with a distinction made between memory and nostalgia. A said nostalgia is an excursion from the living present into the dead past; memory, the summoning of the dead past into the into living present. A widow remembers her dead husband and he is there beside her. When Jesus said, "Do this in remembrance of me," he was not prescribing a periodic slug of nostalgia. Rather he was beckoning us to creatively appropriate an open past!

COOPER

The theologian, Paul Tillich, defined a symbol as that which participates in the reality it represents. He was thinking of sacraments. His definition is also true of words. Take the word, "cooper." In ancient times a cooper made barrels for beer. I did not know this until I looked up the word yesterday!

When I think of the word cooper, I think first of Cooper Avenue in Dumont, New Jersey. Until I was in the 7th grade, I lived on the corner of Cooper and Niagara. One vivid memory of those formative years is running my little metal two-peddled grey jeep into a nest of bees in front of a large piece of cement which reads "Cooper." After 80 years the large block of cement is still there and still reads, "Cooper." I recall not wanting to leave my jeep. It was a fine jeep and it was new. At age five I clearly was not thinking about the danger of the swarming bees! My parents had to pull me from the jeep.

A few years ago I read Anderson Cooper's memoir, *Dispatches from the Edge*. The son of Gloria Vanderbilt, Cooper lost his father and his brother. I suspect this is why Anderson is so gifted in interviewing people who have experienced a great loss. As I watch these interviews, I think of Thornton Wilder's words: "in the Lord's army only the wounded can serve."

A few weeks ago in Central Park, New York City, we were made aware of two more people who from birth have carried the name Cooper. Christian Cooper is a bird watcher, a Harvard graduate, a black man. Amy Cooper is a white woman. She was walking her dog in the park. Cooper told her to put a leash on the dog. She was unhappy with this request and threatened to call the police and report that an "African American" man was threatening her.

I believe this incident speaks volumes. Amy Cooper used her privilege as a white woman to wield power over a black man. It is very difficult for many of us to understand what other people feel and experience. What does it feel like to be turned away from a restaurant or a hospital or even a water fountain? What does it feel to be young and black, driving at night, and being stopped by a policeman?

I once heard sentimentality defied as "enjoyment without obligation." The same might be said about "sympathy." It's a rather shallow word. Empathy is much stronger. The next time I hear the word"cooper," I hope my thoughts go deeper than barrels of beer or even a smart looking car made by BMW. When next I hear the word, "cooper" I hope I remember that whereas irritation is a sign of life, irritation to what others feel is a sign of love.

HAPPINESS

Much has been written of late about happiness. It seems we Americans are unhappy—much more so than in previous decades. How so? Psychologists have suggested three reasons:

Our relationships and community ties are weak.

Our expectations are too high.

We are more focused on things like money, fame, and image.

Cell phones, Facebook, and modern technology can easily give the impression other people are happier than we. This projection is as old as the young prodigal son who complains to his father in Luke 15: "This son of yours (not my brother!) runs through your money with women and you kill the fatted calf for him."

For several weeks I've been watching a major renovation a few blocks from our church. The previous owners, active members of our congregation for over 60 years, are now deceased. Their historic borough home was sold in record time. I recall spending much time in this house. I recall the floors in the living room. Dating back to the early 1800s, they were painted red. A vintage oriental rug covered part of the floor. Several children were raised in this small but lovely home. I suspect there was but one bathroom on the second floor. After this very extensive renovation, this house will be twice as large. I have no idea who will live here or how happy they will be. I can only wonder.

On Sunday afternoons while in seminary, I often relished time with members of the church I was serving. Don and his two sons invited me for dinner. Each Sunday we made homemade ice cream. I recall the rock salt and the physical labor involved in churning the cream into something solid and wonderful to the palate. We often grilled steak on the very small patio in the back yard.

All of the homes on Loudon Street off Roosevelt Boulevard were row houses with front porches. I don't recall anyone having air conditioning. Hence much time was spent on the front porch at night. Neighbors knew neighbors. When someone died or put their beloved dog to sleep, neighbors cared and helped thin out the grief.

Fast forward. The children, now college educated, often buy homes with more property. The houses are mostly large with backyard decks, without front porches. Neighbors now wave, if at all, from a safe distance, unrelated to the virus.

Jesus said of a man who built bigger and bigger barns: "This night your soul shall be required of you: then whose shall those things be? So it is with those who store up treasures for themselves but are not rich toward God." I think William James, father of American psychology, was saying much the same when he wrote: "The greatest use of a life is to spend it on something that will outlast it."

I once heard it said that the great tragedy of Judas was not his betrayal of Jesus, dastardly as it was, but that he didn't stay around long enough to see what God could do with human defection. Perhaps one salutary result of this pandemic is we will come to love those simple and holy things which endure when all else passes away.

SCIENCE

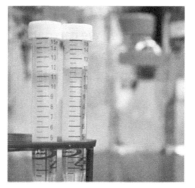

Last week Dr. Anthony Fauci said something we've known for a long time: we suffer in this country from an "anti-science bias." He went on to say "anti-vaxxers" could greatly hinder us from achieving "herd immunity," should we be lucky enough to have an effective vaccine early next year.

Even more pathetic and embarrassing is the way many preachers across our land have joined this "anti-science" bandwagon. Prior to our president's speaking in Tulsa, many evangelical preachers claimed they had a cure for the virus. Thus large gatherings of un-masked people were not to be feared.

A few years ago the Central Bucks West Choir beautifully sang during Sunday worship. After the service, a parent of a choir member chastised me for speaking approvingly of vaccination. The sermon was in fact about being vaccinated by ideas. I only mentioned parenthetically the value of biological vaccination, which in fact has saved millions of lives and spared millions of children from immeasurable suffering. We can rightly thank God for scientists who have used their "God-given skill" to rid this world of terrible diseases and thus make our planet a better place.

Each year I teach our 8th graders that if they want answers to the questions "when" and "how," they would be wise to speak to their science teachers. The religious questions are "who" and "why." The Bible is not a book of science. I like this wise reflection: "The Bible is true and some things happened." Genesis knows nothing of evolution or quantum physics. In fact, any bright fourth grader knows more about science than the Bible, Shakespeare and Luther combined.

When we introduce ourselves to people looking for a church, we state on our brochure the words: "Guided by intellect." I admittedly squirm when churches say they believe the Bible is "infallible and inerrant." I don't know how they can use such language in light of all we have learned from science and biblical scholars over the past century alone! Even Luther did not succumb to such wooden literalism when 500 years ago he said: "The Bible is the manger in which the Christ child lay; we worship the Christ child not the manger."

Great literature has taught us for generations that facts need to be interpreted: something can be eternally true but not literally true. Our great American tale, "The Wizard of Oz," is surely not literally true. Yet what could be more eternally true than to be "saved"—to be whole—means having a heart to feel, a head to think and courage to act!

Please know that I miss very much seeing you each Sunday morning. I long for the day when we can gather together in worship. In the meantime, I hope you are comforted in knowing you belong to a church that, guided by intellect, warms to Albert Einstein's sage advice: "Science without religion is lame; religion without science is blind."

SERENDIPITY

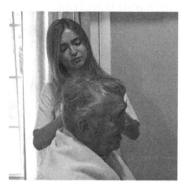

Today I want to explore with you one of my favorite words: serendipity. The word comes from a fairy tale, "The Three Princes of Serendip," the heroes of which were continually finding valuable things by chance, or by sagacity-- things they did not seek. This process of indirection is written deeply into all of life with almost the force of a law.

I noted in a recent sermon a line from *Forrest Gump*: "Life is like a box of chocolates. You never know what you're going to get." He is right! We never expected this pandemic. We never dreamed a year ago that our best scientists would rightly be telling us in this summer of 2020 not wearing a mask is like driving drunk!

Serendipity is finding unexpected treasure as we—much like the Three Princes of Serendip--navigate our way through this world of uncertainty. Emerson said, "Looking for a direct route to Asia, Columbus stubbed his toe on America." Surprise! Jesus said, "Seek the kingdom of God and all these things will be added unto you." Simply put: happiness is not a proper end in itself. It is rather a byproduct of a life that has held steady like a ship at sea to some true course worth sailing. As the old poster has it: "Happiness is like a butterfly. The more you seek it the more it eludes you but turn your attention to other things and it comes and gently sits on your shoulder." Serendipity again!

Several weeks ago I wrote in a blog about Samson, Delilah and the folly of stressing over one's hair. As soon as the essay was published, however, I started fretting over the need for a haircut. It's easier writing about vanity than seeing it in the mirror! By chance I overheard a few of our members talking of how one of our youth Juliet Kennedy—daughter of our recent Director of Christian Education--was attending Cosmetology School. I moved quickly. I offered to come to her house—properly masked--and become her willing and pliant client. I informed her upfront that I had "tributaries of baldness" which appear haphazardly on my head. I added that her challenge would be to skillfully camouflage these tributaries with adroit use of her scissor and comb. I trusted they taught her how to accomplish this feat in one of her cosmetology classes.

It was a delightful afternoon. The whole Kennedy clan was present. They had *Hamilton* on the TV. They served me a fine Pellegrino limoncello seltzer, and I enjoyed immensely catching up on their lives.

I doubt any of this would have happened without this tragic pandemic! I understand Edison serendipitously found a phonograph looking for an electric light. I doubt you or I will do anything so noteworthy, but then again who knows? What I do believe is that God is alive and active in our world of randomness and ambiguity, always eager to cooperate with us in writing straight with crooked lines and transmuting the lead of evil into the gold of growth and blessing.

SCIENCE, PART II - - DIVINITY AND WATERFALLS

Several weeks ago I wrote in a blog about Samson, Delilah and the folly of stressing over one's hair. As soon as the essay was published, however, I started fretting over the need for a haircut. It's easier writing about vanity than seeing it in the mirror! By chance I overheard a few of our members talking of how one of our youth Juliet Kennedy—daughter of our recent Director of Christian Education--was attending Cosmetology School. I moved quickly. I offered to come to her house—properly masked--and become her willing and pliant client. I informed her upfront that I had "tributaries of baldness" which appear haphazardly on my head. I added that her challenge would be to skillfully camouflage these tributaries with adroit use of her scissor and comb. I trusted they taught her how to accomplish this feat in one of her cosmetology classes.

It was a delightful afternoon. The whole Kennedy clan was present. They had *Hamilton* on the TV. They served me a fine Pellegrino limoncello seltzer, and I enjoyed immensely catching up on their lives.

I doubt any of this would have happened without this tragic pandemic! I understand Edison serendipitously found a phonograph looking for an electric light. I doubt you or I will do anything so noteworthy, but then again who knows? What I do believe is that God is alive and active in our world of randomness and ambiguity, always eager to cooperate with us in writing straight with crooked lines and transmuting the lead of evil into the gold of growth and blessing.

I confess I was pleasantly surprised to learn there were 700 views of my recent blog on science! Previously my dog blog was in first place. No more! Why such an interest in science among church people? Let's dive in! My guess is many of us have been told science and religion are an odd couple and just don't get along. The point of viewing determines the point of view.

If we view the world through the lens of science, there is no room for God. If we view the world only through the lens of the Bible, we are forced to compartmentalize our religion and ignore science. Such was the case last week when a pastor in Oregon spoke: "If God wants me to get the virus, I will get it; if God does not want me to get the virus, I will not get it." I was appalled.

I believe such thinking is deadly for the church and the world. John Polkinghorne, a leading quantum physicist and Anglican theologian, is fond of using an illustration Georgetown theologian, John Haught, shared with us a few years ago when he spoke at St. Paul's. Imagine a tea pot with boiling water. Why is the water boiling? One answer is molecules are expanding. Another answer is I turned on the flame. A third answer is my wife wanted tea. All three answers are correct but obviously the answers reveal multi-layers of meaning.

Scottish Bishop and theologian, Richard Holloway, illustrates the same point in a recent book. He says, "You could rightly describe Elgar's 'Cello Concerto' as the rubbing of horsehair over catgut, but while that description would be accurate as far as it went, you'd lose its essence, its soul." Wow. Spot on.

A purely materialistic interpretation leaves many of us cold, painfully aware something important is missing. I believe what's missing is any intimation of purpose or meaning. The writers of Genesis, to be sure, had no interest or knowledge of natural selection and evolution. These are concerns of science. What science cannot answer is *why* the universe exists *and* whether the universe has a purpose in existing or is totally the result of chance--random accidental collocations of atoms.

Ten years ago atheist scientists questioned the appointment of Francis Collins as the Director of the National Institutes for Health. Collins' credentials as a physician and geneticist are impeccable. Yet his appointment was challenged because Collins said he was a Christian and went on to say he had an experience of God's presence while observing a waterfall in the Cascades.

Collins never implied for a second he was seeing a different waterfall than anyone else. What he was saying was the waterfall became *for him* a sacrament, something of molecules reminding him of something not made of molecules—a visible sign of an invisible grace.

Well, ten years have passed and Collins remains a blessing to all of us. I see him each night on television, along with Dr. Fauci and other scientists, helping us navigate our way through this perilous pandemic. Perhaps Krister Stendhahl, Swedish Bishop and Dean of Harvard Divinity School, deserves the final word: "Religion is poetry plus, not science minus." Amen!

COMPLIMENTS AND BEER

Last week at Wegman's I bought a "Craft Your Own Six Pack." Each bottle was unique. As I arrived with my groceries and beer, the young, college-aged cashier requested my driver's license. It's a requirement when buying beer!

Without missing a beat she entered my eight digit number—never looking twice at my license. Awed by such skill, I spontaneously quipped, "You're amazing!" Yes, in preparing a sermon, I can remember quotes from a book I haven't read in years, but I am utterly helpless when it comes to remembering a telephone number seconds after you tell me the number. My compliment was sincere and without guile!

The young lady immediately blushed and said, "Oh, it's just my short term memory. I will forget the number as soon as you leave." Perhaps she wanted to put me at ease and not leave the store thinking she had my driver's license permanently embedded in her encyclopedic memory. My guess is her response revealed something deeper. Most of us have a hard time accepting a compliment!

When we accept a compliment, we give the one offering the compliment a certain amount of power over us. Imagine I say, "That's a lovely color you are wearing." If you unabashedly accept the compliment, you are vulnerable if next week I say, "The colors you are wearing really clash." It is not so easy to dismiss my critique once you accept my praise!

Communication is tricky business. All through life we balance intimacy and distance. To love is to be vulnerable and to be vulnerable means opening oneself to pain. Distance, on the other hand, is a way of avoiding pain but at the price of loneliness and isolation.

I think of a soldier who was dying on the battlefield. The chaplain prayed with him. The soldier said, "I am not sure I believe in God." The chaplain replied, "Ah, that may be so, but God still believes in you!" Once we "accept the fact we are accepted," as theologian Paul Tillich put it, then we are free to live boldly, accepting compliments and giving compliments confident that the mercy of God is greater than our capacity to mess up. This is the gospel—good news indeed!

LIMITATIONS

In my last blog I mentioned buying a "Craft Your Own Six Pack" of beer at Wegman's. I did not mention part of the attraction for me is a counselor, who is present to guide me in selecting the six bottles! The same is true with Tire Rack. You call a toll free number and a counselor guides you in selecting the best tires for you, seeing to it the tires arrive the next day at whatever destination you choose. The counselor will ask you: "Where do you live? What car do you drive? How do you drive? Do you drive in snow?"

The same is true with certain wine clubs. The counselor has you on file and says: "You like New Zealand Sauvignon Blanc. Perhaps you'd like to try this Pinot Gris from Oregon or this dry Riesling from Chile?" Each time you call, the counselor—having your previous order on file--guides you in gently expanding your comfort zone.

Some of you may say, "I don't need a counselor!" Fair enough, but I suggest going it alone is not always a wise way to go. Recently a pediatrician detected what looked like a possible cyst in my granddaughter's eye. I called a good friend from high school who is a professor of ophthalmology in Florida. David's specialty is glaucoma. Without hesitation David said pediatricians don't know much about eyes and suggested we see--not only an ophthalmologist--but a pediatric ophthalmologist!

We took David's advice and were relieved to learn a tuft on the pupil is nothing to fear. Years ago I played tennis with an internist. Tony told me he had no hesitation referring a patient to a cardiologist but a cardiologist may hesitate referring a patient to another cardiologist. Tony said: "Sometimes pride mars our decisions!"

My take on all this is that in an age of increasing specialization it's important to own our limitations. Deborah Tannen, Georgetown Linguist, says men are more guilty here than women. She says men, if lost while driving, are much less likely to ask for directions than women!

I believe our mission statement goes about as deep as one can go on this topic: "We believe through baptism that our worth is a divine gift not a human achievement." True enough. Frankly, I know very little about beer, tires and wine but God loves me no less. Good news indeed—and liberating!

THE SECOND MILE

Last year I discovered a fine butcher in the Poconos. His meatloaf is amazing: a delicious mix of pork, veal, beef, onion and spices all ready for the oven in a ready to cook foil two pound container! The homemade nitrate free link sausage is also worth the trip. We've had a few good steaks and baked lima beans as well. However, a few weeks ago I bought an iron steak. It did not smell good when I put it on the grill and still did not smell good when we were ready to eat it.

When next I returned to the butcher for the legendary meatloaf, in as gentle and disarming way possible, I shared my unhappy experience with the iron steak. I was met with a defensive: "We cut those steaks fresh every morning!"

Driving home I thought of L.L. Bean and Costco and their policy of taking back just about anything. The customer is always right! Correct? To be sure, those with generous return policies have lost money. Customers can be greedy. As in life, if you risk being vulnerable, there will always be those who will take advantage of you! On the other hand, think of all the good will generated by their policy of no questions asked. Consider a preacher who, having a good experience, will use his pulpit to sing your praises and extol your good will. In the end, magnanimity is the winner.

I wanted to share this wisdom with the butcher, but with a line of masked customers I felt it best to move on. I thought of the antonym of magnanimous: pusillanimous. In John Osborne's play, *Look Back in Anger*, there is this caustic putdown: "Behold the lady pusillanimous."

Why is it so hard to be magnanimous—to have a "big heart"? Building on Freud, Erich Fromm suggests the "hoarder" feels he only has a "fixed quantity of strength, energy or mental capacity and that this stock is diminished by use and can never be replenished. He cannot understand the self-replenishing function of all living substance. The act of creation is a miracle of which he hears but in which he does not believe. Mine is mine and yours is yours."

Of course, our Scriptures gave us this sage counsel thousands of years before Freud and modern psychology. Two passages come to mind: "If someone compels you to go one mile, go with him two." (Matthew 5: 41). Or, who can forget the words of St. Paul, our patron saint, in his letter to the Romans: "If your enemy is hungry, feed him, by doing this you will heap coals of remorse upon his head." (Romans 12:20)

To love is to be vulnerable--opening oneself to pain and rejection. There are always those eager to take advantage of you. True enough, but not to love is to experience the pain of isolation and loneliness. Better to aim high and lose rather than aim at nothing and hit it. So, my final word to all you butchers out there: If a customer claims you sold a bad steak, go the second mile and give the customer two steaks! Chances are such magnanimity will reward you in spades!

THE PROPHETIC CHALLENGE

Last week Milo Morris, the bass in our quartet, made headlines in our local paper. He was interviewed at a Black Lives Matter rally here in town wearing a red Make America Great Again hat. Miles is a Black man and this no doubt caught the attention of reporter JD Mullane, whose columns consistently fall right of center.

Milo told Mullane, "Fatherless homes are a bigger threat to black lives than police brutality, which of course exists." In the same paper, it was reported that a Black Lives Matter founder spoke of their being "trained Marxists," and the BLM network speaks of "breaking up the nuclear family model in favor of 'villages' that collectively care for one another." On the same page, Trader Joe's pushed back when accused of racism in their ads for Mexican food.

After digesting these articles, I was reminded of why as a congregation we refuse to identify with either extreme! Yes, I am aware we are called to be prophetic—to speak truth to power and side with the oppressed. The Bible is clearly on the side of the oppressed. No reputable scholar would deny this.

Ernest Campbell, my chief mentor in preaching, once preached a sermon titled, "The Case of Reparations." He preached the sermon the Sunday after a Black militant disrupted the service at Riverside Church in NYC. Campbell's point was that whereas the Good Samaritan only *found* his victim in a ditch, we put ours there! Any honest student of American history knows this to be the case. Segregation has been rampant in our land. In nearby Levittown, Blacks were systemically banned from buying homes. The evidence of racism in our land is overwhelming.

There is no question that what we have done to Blacks in this country is beyond payment in dollars and cents. We have unfamilied them, we have depersonalized them. The challenge is how to help. Defunding police makes little sense in a nation where looters destroy property. On the other hand, we now know police unions protected Derek Chauvin, the officer who killed George Floyd—knowing full well Chauvin had has 18 violations against him! Who can deny that major police reform is needed? Who can deny that unions often are part of the problem, not part of the cure?

Yes, Charles Dickens painted grim pictures in his novels of children being exploited, and we can be grateful for unions that protect the weak and vulnerable. But when unions become powerful, we are wise to remember Lord Acton's words: "power corrupts and absolute power corrupts absolutely."

In short, I believe it is possible to be prophetic without being partisan in our positions. The role of the church is to edit a culture not reflect it. I believe Billy Graham's great weakness was allowing politicians to use him for their own purposes. At the end of his life, he lamented this failure. Would that his son, Franklin, had learned from him! Many preachers on the left have made the same mistake.

I believe one of the great challenges of life is making subtle distinctions. To be prophetic is our calling as a church; to be politically partisan is to succumb to the blindness of knowing more answers than questions. In the end, nail prints speak louder than words. This is the model John Lewis embodied on a Selma bridge half a century ago and embodied still at the end of his life when he challenged us to get into "good trouble." What is good trouble? There is no easy answer! Beware of those who answer the question too soon. As Emily Dickinson wrote: "The Truth must dazzle gradually, /or every man be blind." On the other hand, beware of those who don't answer soon enough. When we sense God is calling us, may we have the courage to act, or as John Lewis put it: "When you see something that is not right, not just, not fair, you have to speak up."

When people ask about our future as a congregation, I like to lift up our brochure which reads: grounded in tradition, guided by intellect, growing in faith. I know this doesn't say it all, but it says much about us and where we want to go in the years to come!

COME TO JESUS

Recently I heard someone use the phrase, "come to Jesus moment." Surprisingly, I never got the impression he meant anything remotely religious. So, I googled the phrase. It goes back to 19th century revivals when, after the sermon, the evangelist would invite sinners to come forward and give their lives to Jesus. Today the phrase has become secularized. Not surprisingly, a handful of people object to the phrase being used in a secular manner void of religious conviction.

I confess I tend to be one of those objecting people. I am not comfortable when someone says, "O my God, my feet are so sore." I was taught the Second Commandment means we do not take God's name in vain. I'm also a stickler with words. Economy of diction is the essence of good writing. E.B. White taught us unnecessary verbiage is a vice. "Now" always trumps "at this point in time."

Lest you think I'm majoring in minors here, let's go deeper. Richard Dawkins, who writes beautifully (by the way), recently suggested the phrase "Black Lives Matter" is nonsense. Dawkins, a famous biologist and militant atheist, went on to say no lives matter! We humans are merely the result of accidental collocation of atoms randomly evolving over billions of years. To think anything "matters" is to engage in wishful thinking.

Secularists tell us a "come to Jesus moment" is a moment of insight--a meeting in which frank, often unpleasant conversation brings to light or resolves an issue at hand. One might respond: "Why bother if nothing matters?" Full disclosure: I'm a preacher. You will thus expect me to say a "come to Jesus moment" without Jesus is a rather hollow affair. Yes, I believe in Darwin's theory of Evolution, but when I see a nine-year-old boy defend his sister from an attacking dog, I don't think of "random collocation of atoms evolving over millions of years." When I see someone drink hemlock rather than betray convictions, or choose crucifixion for a noble cause, I don't think of Darwin. When beauty is loved for its own sake, I don't think of the biological theory of natural selection. I think of God.

The theologian, John Cobb, says there is a perplexing relation between God, the goodness of life and hope for the future. He writes at the end of a book on suffering that we cannot experience life as a blessing if we have no hope. We cannot have hope unless we believe in God. We need all three, and if we break the chain at any point, the whole will dissolve.

I have little in common with those "old sawdust evangelists." I find little to like in their approach, their music or their understanding of science and Scripture. I do agree with them, however, that a "come to Jesus" moment without Jesus leaves one cold.

EDUCERE

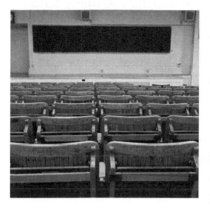

Many of our members here at St. Paul's know Pastor Rusert loves the writings of Franciscan priest Richard Rohr. I've never mentioned Rohr--one infatuation on the pastoral staff is enough! However, after reading several articles recently on education, I stumbled on a quote by Rohr too good to ignore. Rohr writes: "The only thing more dangerous than individual ego is group ego."

Pico Iyer, the author of this essay in *The New York Times*, tells of a college classmate who went to Mass every Sunday precisely because he had no religious commitment. He wanted to learn about perspectives other than the ones he knew. He was startled by the open-mindedness of a devout roommate with whom he argued through the night. He mused: "If someone of a religious faith could be so responsive to other positions, should not a secular liberal aspire to the same?"

Last week I read an article in *The Wall Street Journal* titled, "Bad Teaching is Tearing America Apart." It appears that the current fashion is for teachers to be "guides on the side" rather than "sages on the stage." The essay states that both history and neuroscience explain how education went wrong. It began in the 1940s when schools unbolted the desks and kids were no longer facing the teacher.

A recent study on baseball shows that kids who knew more about how baseball was played performed better when answering questions about a text on baseball than those who didn't understand the game—regardless of their reading level.

Over the past few years, I have been invited on several occasions to give a lecture at North Penn High school to a large group of AP English students because, I was told, many of them have "never heard a lecture."

My conclusion is that Fr. Richard Rohr is right: group ego is dangerous! Our schools are exactly the place to expose students to ideas which disturb them and challenge their views about themselves and the world. Colleges are wise to invite speakers who represent varied and contradictory points of view. The very word *education* comes from the Latin root (*educere*) meaning "to lead out" and thus is the antithesis of indoctrination. Bernard Shaw once quipped that a "Catholic education is a contradiction in terms."

Fortunately, this is no longer true of many Catholic schools today. Yet, truth be told, far too many schools stifle hot and controversial topics resulting in what Richard Rohr calls "group ego" - a form of tribalism which fails miserably in helping students perceive that for every truth there is an opposite truth. Sadly, there are many who—incapable of standing uncertainty—drive themselves toward a certainty that is far worse than the tension they could not bear.

Even in theology, I believe every heresy is a partial truth blown out of proportion. Better to understand the kernel of truth in the "heresy" before dismissing it. Once we understand a topic, then it's time to unbolt the desks, sit in a circle, and let the sparks fly--knowing, as John Henry Newman reminded us a century ago, that "a great memory does not make a mind any more than a dictionary is a piece of literature."

OREGON

Oregon has been on my mind. Mike, my college roommate, grew up—as did I—in the shadow of New York City. After graduation, Mike packed his car and drove west. He worked in Salem and later in Portland. For years he had a small apartment directly on the Pacific Ocean in Lincoln City. He loved Oregon and enjoyed lecturing around the state on his favorite film, Hitchcock's *Vertigo*. We took many trips up and down the coast, enjoyed Shakespeare festivals in Ashland, boat rides on Crater Lake, and white-water rafting on the Klamath and Rogue rivers.

Mike taught me how to pronounce "Oregon" properly lest I embarrass him and sound like a tourist. Mike died a few years ago and I feel the need today, on his birthday, to offer a few reflections on the current state of things in Oregon. Why so many fires? Those on the left seem to talk only about climate change. Those on the right blame excessive regulations, buildup of excess timber, and logging restrictions.

What I find so sad and frustrating is the inability of either side to express the other side's position adequately and empathetically. The same is true with violence and the need for social justice. My grandparents owned and ran a grocery store in Jersey City for 50 years. They worked long hours, often seven days a week. I can only imagine how they would have felt if vandals destroyed their property.

The police officer who killed George Floyd had 18 violations against him. Yet police unions have defended him. Those on the extreme left respond by demanding we defund our police forgetting our need for safe streets; those on the extreme right respond by demanding law and order forgetting you don't cure measles by rubbing off the spots. If the causes remain, the symptoms will reappear, in even more virulent form.

Marriage counselors say in unison that the mark of authentic communication is expressing the feelings of one with whom you differ to that person's satisfaction before speaking! We say blue, blue, blue. We mean yellow, yellow, yellow. What is heard is green, green green. Communication is hard work. It takes courage!

I believe Scott Fitzgerald was right: "The test of a first-rate intelligence is the ability to hold two opposed ideas in mind at the same time and still retain the ability to function." I suspect most people would say they believe in the power of positive thinking and having the courage of one's convictions. Ah, but is it not also true that positiveness is a virtue only if your goal is positive? Why do so many who have the courage of their convictions not have better convictions?

I leave you with this wonderful quote from Oliver Cromwell: "I beseech you in the bowels of Christ to think it possible you may be mistaken." Written in 1650 to the assembly of the Church of Scotland, such humility would go a long way in healing our bruised and broken world!

BIRTHDAYS

September is the month I think of birthdays. My wife's birthday is September 17. My predecessor, Pastor Wilson Hartzell and our longtime clerk, Amy Funk, were born on September 17. Long before I knew either Wilson or Amy, however, birthdays in September were on my radar. Mike, my college roommate, was born on September 21. Bill, a dear friend for over 50 years, was born on September 28. I was born on the 29th. Each September, the three of us outdid each other with clever cards. After Labor Day, the search for the right card began.

Sadly, the competition for the cleverest card is over. Mike and Bill both died a few years ago. Mike was fond of the Frank Sinatra song, "The September of My Years." Sinatra captures flawlessly the melancholy sadness of the song --the pathos that comes when we look back on days that are no more—"the springs and winters of a lifetime, whatever happened to them all?" The hymn gets it right: "Time like an ever-flowing stream bears us all away; we fly forgotten as a dream dies at the opening day." In her late 80s my mom told me: "These are the golden years, but they're tarnished." She had lost so many close friends—13 in one year. She knew I did not really understand the depth of her loss any more than she, at my age, understood the depth of her mother's loss. My mom also knew my experience would mirror hers soon enough. She was right. Woody Allen quipped: "I don't mind dying; I just don't want to be there when it happens."

Is there a lesson to be learned here? Robert Herrick, the 17th century English poet, thought so when he penned his well-known words: "Gather ye Rose-buds while ye may, Old time is still a- flying. And this same flower that smiles today tomorrow will be dying." Some use his words to justify a profligate and hedonistic search for pleasure. It would be foolish and ultimately self-destructive to take this route. Better to simply acknowledge that the race, even at its longest, is short. Hence it is wise to give our flowers to the living. If there is a kind word you can say today, a note you can write, a call you can make, a token of appreciation you can pass on—do not delay!

Jesus told a story about a man who kept building bigger barns. He kept storing up earthly treasures for himself, but God warned him: "You fool, this night your soul will be required of you and whose will all these things be?" It's been said the secret of life is to give it away to something that will outlast it. To live as if we were dying gives us a chance to experience real presence. Life and death are of one piece. Coming full circle, I take my cue from T.S. Eliot:

What we call the beginning is often the end
And to make an end is to make a beginning
The end is where we start from.

TURNING THE PAGE

Last week an author I know in Florida asked me to enter a contest by writing a short story on the topic, "Turning the Page." I don't know if I will write that story. I'm more at home writing essays and crafting sermons than writing short stories. Yet that phrase, "Turning the Page," captures my imagination. What shall we make of it?

The modern poet, Mark Strand, wrote a poem which he titled, "The Next Time." He writes:

Nobody sees it happening, but the architecture of our time
Is becoming the architecture of the next time...
It could have been another story, the one that was meant
Instead of the one that happened.

The poem is as universal as it is personal. If only..... Each of us can take off from these two simple words. Mark Strand wonders to what end? Some neuroscientists say we have no choice. Nature and nurture determine our every move. As the Stoic philosopher Seneca wrote, "Fate leads the willing while the unwilling get dragged."

Assuming we have power--at least in part—to shape our destiny, to what end? Imagine a man marries, has a child, and goes through a divorce. Yes, it "could have been another story...instead of the one that happened." If he had gone to a different college, married a different woman, his life would have been different. He will never know in what way it would have been different, but he knows that if he had taken a different path, the offspring of his broken marriage would never exist. Such a possibility is the last thing he wants to imagine!

Yes, "the architecture of our time is becoming the architecture of the next time." This is the way it is. As we turn the page, we can lament the failures of days gone by, or we can make the most of the new day.

Several years ago, the wrong salt was spread on our cement walkways at church. It was winter. Our contractor thought he was getting rid of the ice. The mistake ruined our walkways but gave us an opportunity. These past few Sundays, hundreds of us have delighted in the flowers adorning our new entrance.

This "new architecture" reminded me of Enterprise, Alabama. If you visit Enterprise, you will find in the town square a statue to a Boll Weevil. A statue in the middle of town to a cotton eating bug? Yes! What appeared to be tragic was a blessing. It forced the people of Enterprise to change their primary industry from cotton to peanuts. Seen in retrospect, this was providential. Hence the statue.

Turning the page is an invitation running all through the Scriptures. Isaiah has God say, "I am doing a new thing." The only time God speaks in the book of Revelation, the last book in the Bible, God says, "I make all things new." May it be so for us! As the poet Robert Browning wrote: "the best is yet to be—the last of life for which the first was made."

CHARLES MOORE, 1929 - 2020

I've known the name "Charlie Moore" since I was a child. He came to Cornell 12 years after my dad graduated. They had the same coach, shared the same locker room, lived in the same fraternity. Charlie was the greater runner. He was in fact the greatest runner in the school's history! Olympic champion, world record holder, never defeated in the 400-meter hurdles. He told Cornell officials years later he would be their athletic director for only five years. In those five years he transformed the athletic department fulfilling his promise to be an agent of change. In business he was CEO of several companies. He was a legend in his own time.

Charlie led our men's retreat at Eagles Mere a few years ago and the men loved him. My relationship with Charlie grew over the years. We moved on quickly from talking about my dad to talking about every topic imaginable. Charlie's wife of 49 years, Judith, is an organist in the Episcopal Church and the archivist at St. Thomas Church, NYC. Our love for good sacred music became a bond. Debbie got along famously with both Charlie and Judith and that only helped the friendship to grow.

When the four of us met for lunch in August, Charlie was dealing with pancreatic cancer. He chose to decline treatment. He said at 90 he did not want to prolong his life a few months if such prolonging meant less quality. I have a photo of our last few seconds together. Judith went to get the car, but Charlie took off after her. No way was he going to wait for her to pick him up.

How utterly strange is death! I cannot believe our consciousness is nothing more than physical cells—chemistry and dust, a mere collocation of atoms. At our lunch in August, I mentioned in passing that I felt the secret of life is to die young as late as possible. Charlie e-mailed a few days later and wanted to hear that quote again. I told him he embodied it more than anyone I had ever met!

I have often said in sermons that those we have loved and lost are our "balcony people"—cheering us on. I believe, as the prayer book felicitously puts it, that the dear friends we have lost are part of the "company of heaven," afflicting us when we get too comfortable and comforting us when we are afflicted. I will never forget our last meal in August. Yes, in a strange way, Charlie enabled me to get closer to my dad.

It didn't take more than one lunch, however, and our friendship had a life all its own. Charlie was a world class athlete, but he was also as kind and authentic a human being as I have ever met. In the words of the prayer book he loved, "may he go from strength to strength in the nearer presence of God." I can't imagine him any other way.

LILY, LAWRENCE AND JESUS

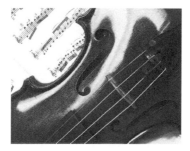

This past week one of our members forwarded to me a fine essay by an English professor at Boston College. In his essay Professor Carlo Rotella makes a persuasive plea for studying literature and gives high praise to Edith Wharton's novel, *House of Mirth*, written in 1905. Inspired by his praise, I quickly dusted off my copy and read again this classic work.

The central theme of the novel is freedom. Lily Bart is captive to the mores of her culture. As a woman in New York society, she sees only two paths to freedom: marriage or money. Wharton says, "Lily might be incapable of marrying for money, but she is equally incapable of living without it." Lawrence Selden talks much about freedom, but he too is a victim of his environment. Edith Wharton says he suffers from "spiritual fastidiousness." He loves Lily but lacks the courage to move from a detached observer to a vulnerable player. Yes, at the last he gets in touch with his better self, but he is too late. Aristotle, in his *Poetics*, speaks of recognition as a major part of tragedy. Edith Wharton unpacks this truth with consummate skill.

Jesus says in John's gospel, "you shall know the truth and the truth shall make you free." This is the Gospel for Reformation Day, which we celebrated this past Sunday. In Wharton's novel, Lily Bart echoes Pilate's question: "What is truth?" She goes on: "Where a woman is concerned, truth is the story easiest to believe."

I suggest this is the soft belly of ethical relativism. Historian Herbert Butterfield was aware of this danger in his seminal work, *Christianity and History*. He writes: "There is a principle which both gives us a firm Rock and leaves us the maximum elasticity for our minds. The principle: Hold to Christ and for the rest be totally uncommitted."

In grammar school I played the violin. I learned quickly that only when the strings are "bound" can there be music. So too in life. The Scottish poet/preacher, George Matheson, captured this truth in his hymn: "Make me a captive Lord and then I shall be free." Freedom is the prize of commitment. Another Scottish preacher, Peter Marshall, put it this way: "Freedom is not the right to do as we please; it is the opportunity of pleasing to do what is right."

The central message of our faith is that we are not accepted by God because we are perfectly acceptable; we are accepted by God because we are perfectly loved. Ah, if only Lawrence Selden had this "Rock" –this recognition--as his firm foundation, perhaps he would not have uttered his word of love to Lily a day too late!

SPEEDY BEATIE DEUTSCH OF ISRAEL

"Speedy" Beatie Deutsch is a world class marathoner from Israel. She was featured last week in the *Wall Street Journal* and likened to Eric Liddell, the Scottish sprinter, who refused to run in the 100-meter trials in the 1924 Olympics because the event fell on a Sunday. Liddell, a devout Presbyterian, switched events and won the 400-meter dash to the surprise of many. The film, "Chariots of Fire," lifted for millions the commitment of this superb athlete who, after the Olympics, gave his life as a missionary in China.

A few thoughts about marathon mother "Speedy Deutsch." First, note her surname! It was a false and demonic form of nationalism which led to the death of millions of Jews in German concentration camps. How ironic that this 31 year old petite 4'11" athlete—who gave birth to five children in six years—has been carrying the flag of her native Israel with a surname meaning "German." When she runs, she prays her passion for running will be a positive witness to a world suffering every day from small minded tribalism! Run, Speedy Deutsch. We wish you Godspeed!

Note next her modesty. When she races, she wears an over-the-knee skirt, long-sleeved jersey and head covering. She is humble about her appearance and not at all judgmental of those who wish to wear less clothing while running. With self-deprecating humor, she speaks of the danger of getting wet while running lest she end up carrying the weight of the water for 26 miles!

We would do well to make a case for modesty. In Genesis we read Adam and Eve clothed themselves with fig leaves to cover their nakedness. Obscenity is the exposure of what is meant to be clothed in mystery. The Bible says darkness covered the earth from the 6th to the 9th hour the day Jesus was crucified. This led one commentator to note this was so no one present could go home and say they saw it all. We would not want to crash the windows of a cathedral to let in more light. Mystery and humility are inseparable. The theologian Daniel Day Williams, in his classic work on the Nature of Love, writes: "An exploitive sexual relationship stupefies the spirit. Its result is insensitivity to the depth and glory of personal communication." The word "stupefy" means: "dull the senses, to be numb." Fig leaves have their place! Speedy Deutsch, thank you for reminding us!

Finally, Speedy Deutsch teaches us the importance of committing ourselves to something bigger than ourselves. Eric Liddell would not compete in the 100-meter Olympic trials on a Sunday. Sandy Koufax would not pitch the first game of the World Series on Yom Kippur. Speedy Deutsch says she will not run in the next Olympic marathon if the event is scheduled on the Sabbath.

The poet, Heinrich Heine, once stood with a friend before a great Gothic cathedral. The friend said, "Heinrich, why can't we moderns build cathedrals like this anymore?" Heinrich replied: "The people who built those cathedrals had convictions. We moderns only have opinions. It takes more than opinions to build a great Gothic cathedral. I hope they change the day of the marathon in the 2021 summer Olympics in Tokyo next summer! If so, I know who I will be cheering to win! Go, Speedy Deutsch! Run to win! *Soli Deo Gloria*--Run to the glory of God!

SERENDIPITY, HAWTHORNE AND CHOCOLATE CAKE

Last week my daughter, Brooke, celebrated her 30th birthday. I'm usually not big on chocolate cake but this was Brooke's birthday, not mine! However, as Shakespeare said, "All's well that ends well." It was an amazing chocolate cake my son-in-law engineered for our celebration. I quickly requested a large piece to take home. I had another piece the following day after lunch. High praise from someone not big on chocolate!

A few days later, by chance, driving home from a wedding in Lewisburg, my wife and I stopped at the "Novel Baker" in Dublin as I was eager to see what else might tempt me. We met Alexis, the creator of this chocolate delicacy. Wondering what her training was, Alexis shared that she had two degrees in English and then switched to science and it was her work in science that lit her interest in baking. She told me she had written a thesis for one of her English degrees on Hawthorne's *The Scarlet Letter*. I told her I had given a lecture at North Penn High School last year on this very novel and would send her a copy if she shared with me her thesis. As we celebrated Brooke's birthday, we would never have guessed any of this! One thing leads to another. This is what makes being alive so special!

Two thoughts. The first is the importance of following your passion. Hawthorne said as much when he wrote: "A single dream is more powerful than a thousand realities." He also wrote: "Happiness is not found in things you possess, but in what you have courage to release." How blessed are those who get paid for doing what they love. I asked the "Novel Baker" many questions about her new career. It became clear to me she loves what she does. A social worker once asked a coal miner in West Virginia if he found his work boring. Picking up a piece of coal, he said: "Not at all, this is light for churches and heat for hospitals." How fortunate to find a doctor, a dentist, a grocer, a teacher, a baker who knows the true meaning of vocation is where you are most needed and where you most want to be meet.

My second thought is about evangelism. Many people in our culture are turned off by organized religion. My favorite definition of evangelism goes like this: "It's one beggar telling another beggar where to find the bread." The "Novel Baker" knows what I do for a living. She also knows I made no attempt to push any political or theological agenda on her. We met her simply as fellow travelers on life's journey—one who shares her passion for food and literature.

For the moment is it not blessing enough when two fellow travelers are able to look outward in the same direction and take delight in so doing? Some would call this luck; I prefer to call it grace.

FAUCI'S ACCENT

I like Dr. Tony Fauci. He is a world class scientist, respected by the best and brightest on both sides of the aisle. In the days to come we will sorely need his guidance, integrity, and wisdom. However, when I hear him speak, it is not the Covid, masks, physical distance, handwashing or vaccines that hit the web of my mind and sticks. It is the man's accent! The man grew up in the "area." By the "area," I mean the New York City area. When I went off to college, and people spoke like Fauci, we knew they were from the area.

The New Yorker Magazine had a famous cover portraying New York City followed by the rest of the country. New York City took up half the cover followed by the next 3,000 miles! My parents were both born in Jersey City and sounded like Fauci. I too spoke like Fauci until I went off to college. I had difficulty pronouncing the letter "s." Fortunately my home pastor's wife was a speech therapist and noticed my bilateral lisp. She helped me learn to use my tongue correctly, moving quickly from "t" to "s." Prior to her intervention, I spent hours practicing lines like "Sally sipped a sarsaparilla soda." I even developed a slight Scottish accent listening to the Scottish preacher, Peter Marshall. I never mastered the skill of rolling the letter "r" like a true Scotsman, but at least I didn't ignore the letter "r" like my parents and Dr. Fauci and millions of others born in the area.

In the Passion narratives, you will recall the scene where Peter denies Jesus three times. Jesus predicted Peter's denial saying to his impetuous disciple, "Before the cock crows twice thou shalt deny me thrice." Peter warms himself by a fire while Jesus is bound and led to his death. A bystander says to Peter: "You are surely one of this man's disciples. Your accent betrays you."

We hear much about getting back to basics--reading, writing, and arithmetic. Recently Michael Smerconish had a guest on his Saturday show—a historian who spoke of the importance of knowing our American Constitution and giving Civics a more central place in our school's curriculum.

As we move closer to Jesus' birth during this Advent season, I suggest there is nothing more basic to our Christian faith than acquiring a Galilean accent. To be a Christian means living with Christ's accent; and that we can only learn by dwelling much with him. Gradually, imperceptibly, quite unknown to ourselves, we will acquire his accent and we too will begin to love the unlovely, care for those in need, speak truth to power, elevate justice over greed, kindness over indifference. One of my favorite Advent anthems goes like this:

Thou shalt know him when he comes
Not by any din of drums,
Nor his manners, nor his airs,
Not by anything he wears…
But his coming known shall be,
By the holy harmony,
Which his coming makes in thee.

MIRACLES

In Jan Swafford's new book, *Mozart: The Reign of Love*, he writes: "One can believe in miracles as a matter of faith, but one does not expect them to turn up in the living room." He was speaking of Mozart's genius at the age of 3. The word *miracle* surfaces on page after page of this impressive biography.

Did God intervene and give Mozart a miraculous talent? Much of the world believes in reincarnation. Even some Christian theologians have raised the possibility of reincarnation when speaking of Mozart. He must have been a prodigy in his previous life. My biggest problem with reincarnation is that it seems to deny our individuality as we progress from one life to the next.

Miracles are hard to address in our modern world. We know more about science today than those who lived hundreds of years ago. Take, for example, the parting of the Red Sea. Most scholars argue that it was really the "Sea of Reeds." A strong wind dried up the marshy land and the Jews escaped their Egyptian bondage. Pharaoh's charioteers—the most powerful people in the world—pursued the weak and vulnerable Jews but heavy rain poured down from the heavens and their chariots were clogged in the mud.

Was this central event in Hebrew history a miracle? Unbelievers say it was a fortunate coincidence at best. Believers see the hand of God:

Sing to the Lord, for he has triumphed gloriously:
horse and his rider he has hurled into the sea! (Exodus 15: 21)

Jonathan Sacks, chief Rabbi of England who died recently, said in a debate with Richard Dawkins that the exodus was indeed a miracle even though no natural laws were broken. He calls the story a "polemic against power" reminding us of God's powerlessness winning in the end. I would argue that the heart of biblical religion is not loveless power or powerless love but something more wonderful still--the power in love, in love with us!

When we turn to Christmas, we see the same theme: a helpless babe, no room in the inn, a stable —manger power. In the words of Mary's Magnificat: "He hath put down the mighty from their thrones and exalted those of low degree." Such power is persuasive not coercive, underwhelming not overwhelming, stooping, ceasing to be everything so we can be something. The theologian John Hick has written of the need for God to keep distance from us so we can grow up. He speaks of "epistemic distance." Luther speaks of "Deus Obsconditus" –the hidden God. As we read in Exodus 33: "You will see my back, but my face shall not be seen."

Sadly, in our day the word "myth" is linked with "false." I prefer to see a myth as a story that is *always* true— an attempt to answer in dramatic and pictorial language a basic truth of humankind. Ancient stories can be eternally true even when not literally true.

One night long, long ago God came to us and history was split in half over the roof of a Bethlehem barn. He came in great humility and that is the way he always comes. The question before us is whether we will run away in fear or will be brave enough to be open to the questions, the struggles, the hopes of our lives and our world and let God come in—the God who stooped to a stable but whose love is more enduring than the stars.

FAITH

Last week a college friend and teammate texted me at 3 in the morning. He was reading Somerset Maugham's novel, *Of Human Bondage*. He said he couldn't put the book down and wondered what I thought of it.

In this novel, written in 1915, Philip suffers from a clubfoot. His friends at school ridicule him as a cripple. Philip prays fervently for God to heal him, but his prayers are unanswered. This is the beginning of Philip's loss of faith. So too for Maugham. His handicap was stuttering not a clubfoot, but scholars agree that Philip's struggle was Maugham's very own.

Maugham never stopped searching for God and the meaning of human existence, but he never found any convincing answers from the church of his day. He even travelled to India to find meaning in Eastern religions to no avail.

In his Beecher Lectures at Yale, the preacher Paul Scherer commented on this struggle. He wrote: "Relating a clubfoot to God may be the ruin of one's religion. Relating God to a clubfoot may be the making of one's life."

I once heard a banker use the term "frozen asset." A frozen asset is something that at the moment cannot be turned into cash gain, however it ultimately can be turned into cash. So too with suffering. In a later novel, *The Razor's Edge* (1943), Maugham says as much: "Would Byron have been Byron but for his club foot, or Dostoyevsky without his epilepsy?"

People say, "look at the evidence." The trouble is the evidence is ambiguous. In nature there are sunsets and earthquakes. There is a bed of violets by a rippling brook, and there are hurricanes and floods. What is true of nature is also true of history: for every Bach in Leipzig, there is a Hitler in Berlin. The facts are neutral. How we interpret the facts is what matters. The English poet, Robert Browning, put it to us decades before Maugham:

The Grand Perhaps!

We stumble at truth's very test.
All we have gained then by our unbelief
Is a life of doubt diversified by faith,
For one of faith diversified by doubt...
So what think ye of Christ, friend?
When all's done and said,
Like you this Christianity or not?
It may be false, but will you wish it true?
Has it your vote to be so if it can?

WORDS

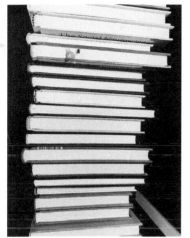

Last week I was saddened to learn Frank Honeycutt would no longer be writing his column in our national magazine, *Living Lutheran*. Simply put: the man is great with words! How easily we forget one needs only a piece of paper, a pen and in an hour the world can be changed. Martin Luther King did not even have a piece of paper in that Birmingham jail when he penned his famous letter. He wrote on scraps of an old newspaper. His namesake, brother Martin--thanks in part to the newly invented printing press—turned the world upside down when he posted his 95 Theses on the door of a Wittenberg church 503 years ago.

Poet T.S. Eliot reminded us: "Words strain, crack, and sometimes break under the burden, under the tension, slip, slide, perish, decay with imprecision, will not stay in place, will not stay…" True enough, yet our broken speech has power. What starts as a sound, ends in a deed.

No wonder millions were moved at this week's Inauguration by the words of 22-year-old poet Amanda Gorman. Frankly, most political talk bores me. It is all so bland and predictable--lacking in precision, economy of diction, grace and power. Yes, every decade or two a politician or speech writer says something worth remembering, but a decade is a long time to wait.

How utterly refreshing when a young Black woman in her 20s, who has struggled with a speech impediment and an auditory processing disorder, stands before a podium at a Presidential Inauguration and wows a nation. What an unexpected gift to a people who, weary of hate and division, long for a word of hope. Gorman's poem skillfully offers just such a word. The entire poem throws down this gauntlet to us: "Our nation isn't broken, just unfinished."

I recall the Georgetown theologian, John Haught, sharing with us the same insight. He asked us to imagine 30 large volumes symbolizing the history of our world from the beginning of time. He then said: "Where do we humans appear in these 30 volumes?" The answer was the last few sentences on the last page of the last volume!

The message was clear: We live in an unfinished world and God calls us to be co-creators with him in making this world a better place. In John 5, Jesus says, "My Father is still working." The world is incomplete. Work awaits our hands and feet. We are in the making still. What we choose is what we are. What we love, we yet shall be.

Thank you, Amanda Gorman! May God grant you the grace to hone your gift and bless us with your words for decades to come.

14

It was Thursday. My last night in Florida and not a cloud in the sky. I knew the sun was setting at 6:13 pm. As I made my way to the beach, a man with a sense of urgency blurted out: "You better hurry. You have 14 seconds!" I started running. It was only about 30 yards to the beach. An easy run. I arrived with seconds to spare.

As I left the beach, the number "14" was ringing in my ears. Running a half mile, 14 seconds would take me halfway through the first turn, 28 seconds to the 200 mark, 56 seconds the end of the first lap, 84 seconds the 600 mark and then the test begins: the last and hardest 200 yards. A distant yet vividly familiar memory!

I thought of February 14—Valentine's Day. It will be my turn to preach. How shall I breathe new life into an old word? I thought of Shakespeare's sonnets—each sonnet fourteen lines. In sonnet 14, he speaks of the stars, plagues, of luck good and bad, and the Bard ends on this sober note: "Thy end is truth and beauty's doom and date."

Sober, perhaps, but a blessing, nonetheless. What would a baseball game be without nine innings? What would a fight be without ten rounds? What would life be without death? It is limitation that adds zest and meaning to life. Without death, we'd never live. Without discovering the limits of our talents, we'd never discover who we are. The sun set at 6:13 pm. The man was correct: I had 14 seconds. We can count on this astronomical fact. Tomorrow the time of the sunset will be different, and we can count on that too.

A sonnet would be something quite different and the challenge quite different without the 14-line requirement. Child psychologists have been telling us for years that it is good for a child to have boundaries, limits. Creativity thrives on owning one's finite place in the universe. If you knew you only had 14 minutes or 14 seconds left, what would you do? Who would you call? What would you say? The psychologist, Rollo May, wrote about a man dying of a terminal illness. The man commented: "I never knew the sky was so blue. I never noticed so acutely the soft look in my dog's eyes."

300 years ago, the English writer, Samuel Johnson, famously quipped: "Depend on it, when a man knows he is to be hanged, it concentrates his mind wonderfully." Or, once heard, how can we forget the way Emily Dickinson expressed this truth:

By a departing light
We see acuter, quite,
Than by a wick that stays.
There's something in the flight
That clarifies the sight
And decks the rays.

Deserted by his disciples, in agony on the cross, barely 30 years old, Jesus said, "It is finished," and thus ended the most complete life ever lived. The Ash Wednesday liturgy declares each year, pandemic or no pandemic: "Remember you are dust and to dust you shall return." Ah, but a cross made with ashes tells us there is hope, even in the dust!

"You better hurry. You have 14 seconds." Thank you, sir. I will not forget!

ADMIRATION

I don't know if envy is the right word. Several synonyms come to mind: jealous, begrudge, covet. All I know is that when people say, "imitation is a form of flattery," I know what they mean. We would be less than honest if we did not admit we often see in others gifts we admire. Ah, maybe "admire" is the right word—it doesn't seem as "sinful" as those other words. Let's not forget in this Lententide that two of the Ten Commandments warn us not to covet!

Be all this as it may, while on vacation last year my wife and I discovered a church and preacher in Sarasota, Florida we admire. The preacher comes from LA—Lower Alabama. This Episcopal Church recently called the preacher to be their rector. In his wonderful southern drawl, he began his acceptance speech by confessing: "I'm as nervous as a long-tailed cat in a room full of rocking chairs."

"Wow," I thought. "What a colorful image." So colorful, in fact, that for an hour I tried to imitate his accent, repeating the words to anyone who came close. Fortunately, our Office Manager, Meg Evans, grew up in South Carolina and spoke the needed words: "Face it, you grew up in North Jersey. You will never get it right!"

On the other hand (there's always another hand!), we would be poorer of soul if we did not admire gifts we do not possess. If you desire to be a great violinist, get close to other great violinists. If you want to be a superb sous chef, get close to those who have mastered the art. If you want to be a good preacher, listen to the great preachers of the past. Perhaps something in them will rub off on you.

I'm not talking about plagiarism, which is stealing. The New York preacher, George Buttrick, was once asked how he felt about young preachers stealing his sermons, which each week were printed and could be found in the narthex of his church at 73rd and Madison Avenue. Buttrick beautifully replied: "Well, they can steal my words, but they cannot steal my agony."

When in tenth grade, I admired a fine half-miler at nearby Tenafly High School who warmed up by lifting his knees high in the air. I started doing the same! Attempting to correct a bi-lateral lisp in college, I listened for hours to the sermons of Peter Marshall. In time, I dropped the Scottish accent, but I never lost my admiration for his near perfect diction.

The next time I give a speech in a strange setting and feel nervous, I just may begin with the words: "I feel as nervous as a long-tailed cat in a room full of rocking chairs." You can be sure, however, I will not attempt the accent! In short: coveting, envy, jealousy, begrudging are all sins to be confessed, especially in this Lenten season. However, to admire and give thanks and learn from the gifts of others is, as the prayer book so felicitously put it: "meet, right and salutary."

RESTRAINT

Last week I ordered a clerical collar from a church supply store. On the catalog's cover was a chasuble—the poncho-like vestment the celebrant wears during communion. I groused: "That's the least attractive chasuble I've ever seen." Our Office Manager quickly said: "please don't say that when you order the collar." Pastor Rusert chimed in, "Why don't you write a blog on restraint."

Well, I've had a few days to reflect on the matter, so here goes. First, I believe there is a difference between taste and judgment. There is a difference between playing God and playing dumb. Let's face it: there is good cheese and bad cheese. Not everything is up for grabs. Yes, discriminating against is a bad thing, but discriminating between is why we study music, art, and the culinary arts. Philosophers study aesthetics because they know this to be so.

What, then, is the role of restraint in our day-to-day life? There is an art to handling hot subjects with a cool hand. Perhaps it is wise to begin by asking, "Are the words I'm about to utter helpful or hurtful?" Here are three good questions to get things off dead center: Is what I'm about to say true? Is it necessary? Is it kind? If I can't answer all three questions in the affirmative, perhaps best to practice restraint!

The philosopher, Nietzsche, once wrote that our best friend is our most vigilant critic. True, it is no easy task saying something to another that is both painful and true in a way that builds up rather than tears down. Hundreds of years ago, Alexander Pope warned about "damning with faint praise—without sneering, teaching others to sneer." Such "passive aggression" seldom passes the test of being true, necessary and kind.

Going deeper, I dare say the most difficult topic in theology is suffering which achieves no good end. Philosophers call this dysteliological suffering. On *60 Minutes* last Sunday I watched images of unspeakable torture in Syria. I thought: "why is God's action so restrained? Why doesn't God intervene?" In a new novel titled, *Migrations*, Charlotte McConaghy quotes the poet John Keats: "Do you not see how necessary a world of pains and trouble is to school an intelligence and make it a soul?"

Keats is surely right. We've all observed suffering which helps one become more compassionate, but the suffering in Syria is so unfathomable it is hard to see any good coming out of it. The only response I dare to offer is that love is self-restrictive when it comes to power. Simone Weil, the French mystic, in her work, *Attente de Diu*, put it this way: "On God's part creation is not an act of self-expansion but of restraint and renunciation." God ceases to be everything so we can be something. God becomes weak so we can become strong. God stoops to a stable, coming into the world as a child, so we can grow up.

This divine restraint is central to our faith. We believe when the Son suffers, the Father suffers too—suffers the pain of what Thomas Aquinas called "letting-be." Yes, a grim failure this Jesus was on the cross; but from that day to this it has been better to fail with him than to succeed with the people whose business it is in every generation to nail him there! It is the hope of this Lenten season that kneeling at the foot of the cross we are moved to confess in the words of a beloved hymn: "Love so amazing, so divine, demand my soul, my life, my all."

JAKE'S REMAINS

Last week I spotted a car at a local library in Florida with New Jersey plates. I asked the woman exiting the car where in New Jersey she resides. She replied, "Sussex County—Lake Mohawk." With surprise I said, "My father and grandfather hunted in Maine with a physician from Brooklyn who had a summer home on Lake Mohawk—Jake Sheetz."

Startled, the woman replied: "I knew Jake's children, Andy and Lynn, and we water skied off of the Sheetz dock." Memories—how they come surging back to accuse or to make clean. Drawn in I told the woman: "Let me tell you about Jake's remains. After he died, he wished his ashes to be scattered on Spectacle Pond, adjacent to the hunting camp in Northern Maine—30 miles from the nearest road. Unfortunately, the ash-filled tin can would not sink, and Jake's friends (my dad and grandfather among them) felt they had no choice but to shoot the can so it would sink. They all loved Jake and did not mean to be disrespectful and felt he would have actually enjoyed his final committal."

I think this chance encounter made this woman's day. Yet, as we parted there in the lot of the library, a feeling of loss came over me. I wanted to call my mom, my dad, my grandfather--all those who knew Jake and would remember his strange burial at sea.

In her novel, *Housekeeping*, Marilynne Robinson writes: "Memory is a sense of loss, and loss pulls us after it. It is hard to separate longing from possessing…When does a berry break upon the tongue as sweetly as when one longs to taste it, and when is the taste refracted into so many hues and savors of ripeness and earth, and when do our senses know anything so utterly as when we lack it? So, whatever we lose, craving brings it back to us."

Memory is central to our faith. If nostalgia is an excursion from the living present into the dead past, memory is summoning the dead past into the living present. On the night in which he was betrayed, Jesus blessed the bread and wine and said to his disciples, "Do this in remembrance of me." He was not inviting them--and us--to engage in a slug of periodic nostalgia, singing each week, as it were, with old Bob Hope, "Thanks for the Memories."

Far from it. Faith at its best is a creative appropriation of an open past. To "re-member" is not only to think about something that once happened but by God's grace to be formed anew and have our members re-created for the future. This is our faith. We live to die; we die to live. Or, as John Updike said in his last poem: "Birthday/death day—what day is not both?"

THE THINGLINESS OF THINGS

I believe it was the philosopher Heidegger who first coined the phrase, "The thingliness of things." I think I know what he means. The 18th century Japanese poet, Yosa Buson, wrote:

The piercing chill I feel:
My dead wife's comb, in our bedroom,
Under my heel.

Things matter. Even a broken comb can participate in the reality it represents. Yesterday I moved out of my church office. It was the shortest move I've ever made-20 yards down the hall. (I just paced the distance!) I moved into my former office 43 years ago. An average of 5 hours a day, 300 days a year, times 43 years equals more than 64,000 hours in one room: thousands of sermons crafted, more pain and joy shared in 300 square feet than one could possibly imagine.

I have no illusions I will spend so much time in my new office. I like the new setting: the blue walls, the 1850 farm table, the intimacy of a smaller space. It feels good, yet time goes quickly. Even at its longest the race is short.

In making this move, I've stumbled on photos and letters out of sight for decades. One letter from the Cornell track coach to my grandfather was dated 1933. It seems my dad had rolled over his 1932 Ford driving to Ithaca to begin his freshman year. Coach John Moakley wrote my grandfather, "the boy has a lot of energy and I'm sure training and studies will turn his attention away from this new toy."

There were other old letters and photos in need of a good dusting and a new home. The thingliness of things. Theologians speak of living in a sacramental universe. Bread, wine, water? More than they seem! Yosa Busan lived in Japan over 200 years ago. His poem is called a haiku. Just as a sonnet has a particular form, so too a haiku—5,7,5, structure. Most would not spend a morning studying such technicalities, but the experience Busan shares moves us to tears. We have been there!

The thingliness of things. Yes, you may choose to describe Elgar's Cello Concerto as the rubbing of horsehair over catgut. The description would be accurate as far as it went, but you would lose its essence, its soul. St Paul wrote to the Church at Corinth: "the things that are seen are transient; the things that are unseen are eternal." This is our Easter faith: eternal life is life in the eternal. It can begin today. So bloom, frozen Christians, April stands before your door!

RIPENESS

Harold Bloom, the longtime Yale literary critic, died in October 2019. His last book, completed shortly before his death, is over 600 pages and links the best of English poetry to the reality of death. I was surprised when Bloom admits being puzzled by this line in Shakespeare's *King Lear*:

"Men must endure their going hence even as their coming hither.
Ripeness is all. " (Act V, Scene 2)

I take "ripeness" to mean maturity--the wisdom, insight, humor and humility that comes from a life well lived. The writer of Hebrews says Jesus learned obedience in the "school of suffering." Ripeness is the reward of knowing– often through pain and loss—that what doesn't make for gratitude can make for growth. Gloucester is blinded by his ungrateful children and learns to see "feelingly." (Act IV, scene 6)

One thinks of the late Prince Philip giving up a successful naval career for the sake of his country and his wife. Admiral William McRaven writes of heroes in a new book *The Hero Code*. He mentions meeting "Charlie" at a formal dinner and how impressed he was at the man's humility and grace. Later McKeever asked Roger Staubach, "who was he?" Staubach replied: "Yes, one would never know after talking with him for over an hour that he was the youngest man to walk on the moon." Humility and ripeness go hand in hand.

Sometimes it is easier knowing what ripeness is not. Bloom tells of meeting a literary critic when he was a young man. The critic asked Bloom the theme of his PhD dissertation at Yale. Bloom replied: "Shelley." The critic responded: "I have settled Shelly." To which the brash 24-year-old Bloom retorted: "Shelley always buries his own undertakers." After hearing this retort, the famed critic jumped up and left the room. His wife made a speechless gesture indicating that I was to depart. The tea was quickly over!

Why are some people so thin-skinned? Why was this critic not able to chuckle and press Bloom to elaborate on his admiration for Shelly? Prince Philip was quoted in a recent essay in the Wall Street Journal as saying, "Being offended is part of life."

I recall reading a book on laughter and liberation. The writer, a psychotherapist, tells of a man who threatened to commit suicide by jumping out of the window of the hospital. The therapist asked the distraught young man, "How are you going to do it? A swan dive, in your pajamas or in the raw?" The patient was able to laugh at himself and it was the first step toward his recovery! Ripeness is linked to laughter and laughter is linked to humility—one day we are born and one day we die. We have value because we are loved not loved because we have value.

I think of a preacher in Florida who is rector of a fine church. One day he was venting at the traffic and uttering unkind words. His young daughter quickly brought him down—as only our children can do—when she said from the backseat: "Dad, you're such a great priest." He turned the exchange into an Easter sermon titled: "What do you want to be when you grow up?" He didn't mention Shakespeare, ripeness or King Lear. He did one better. He mentioned a risen Jesus, who reads us down to the basement of our lowest thought and loves us nonetheless. Ripeness indeed!

COMPETENCE

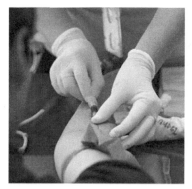

Every few months I donate blood. I do it to help others, and to help myself. I have too much iron and thus giving blood is a win/win.

Over the years I've learned being a good phlebotomist is innate. You have the gift, or you don't. Each time I arrive to give blood, I deliver the same speech: "I have thin veins, lots of scar tissue from frequent donations. I need your best phlebotomist."

Often the phlebotomist ignores me, fails and seeks the help of someone nearby with "the gift." Last week I was startled when, after giving my rehearsed customary speech, the woman in charge disarmed me saying: "All the thin vein people left two hours ago." She then laughed. I was suddenly at ease. She did not exhibit a smidgeon of insecurity. I sensed I was in good hands, ministered to by competence.

I think often of G.K. Chesterton's quip: "If I were drowning, I'd rather an atheist came by who could swim than a bishop who couldn't." Piety is no substitute for competence. Perhaps you've seen the yellow directory listing "Christian merchants." My first thought is: "Great they go to church and love the Lord but are they good?"

The same applies to "bedside manner." Most of us warm to having a dentist, doctor or therapist who has a good "bedside manner." However, if I must choose, I'd give up the bedside manner for competence!

Jesus told a parable (Matthew 25) once about a man with one talent who buried that talent in the ground. He was condemned to "outer darkness where there was anguish and gnashing of teeth." New Testament scholars are one in their belief that we are called to be good stewards of the gifts given to us. "Nice" doesn't quite cut it. The parable implies even God has a hard time forgiving the hanger back.

Shakespeare put it this way: "Our doubts are traitors and make us lose the good we oft might win by fearing to attempt." (*Measure for Measure*, Act 1, scene 4) Fear and faith don't mix well. The preacher, Paul Scherer, tells of Sir Francis Drake's sailors, who used to sit on the rocky coasts of England lecturing the country lads not about the pleasures of the sea but of its dangers. They talked of high waves and stout winds and gallant ships riding out the storms, until those country boys wanted it so much they would run away from home to become part of it.

There is something of that in God. Jesus was sure of it. He waged his life on it. He calls us to do the same. Luther is quoted as saying, "Christian shoemakers do not put little crosses on shoes but make good shoes." At the end of everything he wrote, Bach added: "Soli Deo Gloria—to God alone the glory."

After setting a PR—a pint of blood in five minutes! —I turned to all those present and said, "This woman is the best." She smiled broadly and called after me as I hurried from the gym, "Don't forget your coat."

THITHER

This Thursday, May 13, is Ascension Day. Forty days after Easter, it is a major but neglected feast in the church year. Jesus is let loose in the world, no longer bound by time and space but still closer than breathing and nearer than hands and feet. The traditional Collect for this feast reads: "As we believe our Lord Jesus Christ to have ascended into the heavens; so may we also in heart and mind thither ascend, and with him continually dwell…"

Thither? Where or what does this word mean? The dictionary says, "toward that place, in that direction…hither and thither." The theologian, Reinhold Niebuhr, once wrote that "it does not behoove we mere mortals to conjecture overmuch about the temperature of hell or the furniture of heaven."

Sadly, there are many in our midst who seem to know it all. Our country is terribly divided. A liberal sage was interviewed the other night and was 100% sure unemployment checks do not discourage people from seeking employment. Another sage, this one on the right, was 100% sure the presidential election was stolen, Biden was not really president, and Liz Cheney was a traitor. No evidence can persuade either of these citizens to internalize the truly sage counsel of Lord Cromwell, penned in 1650: "I beseech you in the bowels of Christ, think it possible that you may be mistaken."

Thither may be a word we term archaic, but I like it. I like it because it captures the mystery, wonder and awe of our faith. I don't know anything about the temperature of hell or the furniture of heaven. I do know kindness is better than cruelty, love better than hate, compassion better than indifference. I believe the brightest and best we know to be winsomely incarnate in one carpenter of Nazareth.

This is the heart of my faith. Thus, I try to read each day *The Wall Street Journal* and *The New York Times*. Not one of us has a blueprint for thither. We have notions of the absolute, but we have no absolute notions. I shy away from those who seem to know too much. When on vacation, I seek a church which uses words like "thither" -- elevating mystery, awe and humility over certainty. I hope one day I will "thither ascend," but "for the time being" (to use Auden's phrase) I will do my best to follow here on earth that One who walked this way before me and walked it well-who was the way, is the way, and will be at the end of all our ways!

ACUITY

Three years ago, my vision blurred. After cataract surgery, I had new eyes. 20/15 vision for distance and glasses took care of reading. All this changed recently. Reading became difficult, night driving a challenge. The glare of the sun more pain than pleasure. Instead of taking three pages into the pulpit, I took eleven. The font grew from 11 to 20 overnight.

I was told laser surgery would do the trick. A friend, an eye surgeon in Florida, said, "chances are very good for immediate improvement in acuity." I thought, "a great word—acuity!" It comes from the Latin and means pointed, sharp. A few reflections.

First, science can be a great blessing. My mother was in the hospital ten days after gallbladder surgery. Today she would be in and out in a day. Vaccinations save thousands of lives and spare us much suffering and pain. Luther and Lincoln both stood helpless as they watched a child die of diseases we could treat today. I have little patience for those religious people who say silly things like, "God will take me when my number is up," or "I will not get vaccinated because my life is in God's hands and he will take me when he is ready." I feel much more comfortable with Augustine's take on the matter. 1700 years ago, he wrote: "Without God we cannot; without us God will not." We are co-creators with God in an unfinished world. When my "acuity" improved hours after laser surgery, I thought, "Thank God for science."

My second observation again goes back to Augustine and his doctrine of contrast. These past few months I felt guilty I had taken my good vision for granted. Last week I could not even see the words under the fish at the supermarket. Reading was near impossible without a magnifying glass. Yes, a few months ago I watched a sunset off the Florida coast and uttered a prayer of thanksgiving, but most days I just assumed 20/15 vision was my right and seldom gave it a second thought.

Simone Weil, the French mystic, put it this way: "The sea is not less beautiful in our eyes because we know sometimes ships are wrecked on it. On the contrary, this adds to its beauty." We never appreciate health so much as after we've been sick. I guess in the end we need to decide whether we thank God for roses or curse him for thorns. As Browning said in one of his most thoughtful poems:

All we have gained by our unbelief is a life of doubt diversified by faith,
for one of faith diversified by doubt: we called the chess-board white --we call it black.

When we lose a loved one, we become acutely aware of our loss. Ah, there is that word again! Emily Dickinson used the word better than most—poets usually do!—when she wrote:

By a departing light we see acuter, quite, than by a wick that stays.
There's something in the flight that clarifies the sight and decks the rays.

If you are looking for a biblical text, here it is: "God co-operates in all things for good with those who love him." (Romans 8) Yes, as Jesus said, "the rain shines on the evil and on the good." Randomness often reigns. Yet, in the midst of our uncertainty, we live in hope that ultimately, as the old hymn has it:

Though the cause of evil prosper, yet tis truth alone is strong;
…Behind the dim unknown, standeth God within the shadow,
Keeping watch above his own.

AFFIRMATION

Last week I heard a therapist say during a TV interview that many of her colleagues are fearful of offering any counsel which might be deemed as not "affirming." Language evolves and I have begun of late to question this word affirm. The dictionary defines it thus: "to state as a fact, strongly and publicly. To offer emotional support and encouragement."

Affirmation sounds so warm and fuzzy. I wonder how it squares with the philosopher Nietzsche's observation that "your best friend is your most vigilant critic." Or what shall we make of last Sunday's assigned gospel for Pentecost? Jesus is quoted as saying the Holy Spirit will "prove the world wrong about sin, justice, and judgment." The King James Version says reprove, which means reprimand, censure.

The Holy Spirit does not seem very affirming here! These are strong statements. I recall a graduation speech in which Ted Koppel told the Duke graduates: "We have spent 5,000 years as a race of rational human beings trying to drag ourselves out of the primeval slime. Our society finds truth too strong a medicine to digest undiluted. In its purest form truth is not a polite tap on the shoulder; it is a howling reproach. What Moses brought down from Mt. Sinai were not the Ten Suggestions. They are Commandments. ARE not WERE." He knew if he could get these graduates to say no to anything, who knows what great things they may yet accomplish!

I believe the Holy Spirit "proves some things wrong…" and if we are to discern the Spirit's desires, we would do well to seek out an honest friend–perhaps a few honest friends who will level with us, say "the emperor has no clothes"—and be strong enough NOT to affirm our every impulse.

To quote the British scholar and churchman, Dean Inge: "He who marries the spirit of the age soon finds himself a widower." When in doubt, best to move slowly, pray fervently, and seek out people who do not want your job, your house, your dog or your spouse. It just may be the Holy Spirit will use such blessed friends to help us discern the path we are called to take!

We hear much these days of "grade inflation." Teachers want to "affirm" their students (and parents?). I wonder if excellence is fostered in a culture when every paper gets an "A", and every budding athlete gets a trophy? I think of a teacher who told a student, "John, this paper has real potential. I'd like you to write it over and see if you can improve it."

Recently, cleaning out my office, I found a paper I had written for a professor at Princeton Seminary. He wrote at the end of the paper: "I give your heresy an A, but a B- for the structure and development of your paper." I was not happy reading that comment. I found another paper on which was written: "worthy of publication." Affirmation wears many faces!

THE OTHER HAND

In his always balanced and incisive Saturday morning show, Michael Smerconish reported today homicides in Philadelphia have spiked 30% in the past year. I thought: so much for defunding the police.

I have often told the story of the man who was looking for a one-armed lawyer—one who would not say, "on one hand, on the other hand." Ah, but most truths have two hands. These truths are called paradoxes. Some on the left continue to speak naively about social workers replacing our police. They seldom speak of rising crime and homicides in our cities, protests turning violent, looting, destruction of property.

On the other hand, there are those on the right who refuse to name the insurrection of January 6, preferring to call it an "event." They seldom speak of the need for police reform, or racism and social injustice as a root causes of violence and social unrest.

It was the philosopher, Hegel, who spoke of thesis, antithesis, synthesis. The most insightful minds in human history have echoed this truth. Blake: "Without contraries there is no progression." F. Scott Fitzgerald: "The test of a first-rate intelligence is the ability to hold two opposing ideas in the mind at the same time and still retain the ability to function." Carl Sandburg said of Lincoln: "He was steel in velvet." Jesus urged us to be "wise as serpents, innocent as doves."

I just finished a new book by the neuroscientist, Jamie Wheal, titled: *Recapture the Rapture*. Wheal is critical of religious fundamentalism, which he calls "Meaning 1.0." He has in mind here a literal interpretation of Scripture, a distrust of science, a narrow focus on individual salvation. Wheal believes the sharp decline in organized religion continues to grow rapidly and has caused a vacuum filled by what he calls "Meaning 2.0." Here he speaks of "nihilism"—a total loss of meaning-a blanket dismissal of truths that don't submit to microscopes and telescopes. We end up, Wheal believes, swapping our dusty fundamentalism with a newer, shinier version of the same.

I was wondering where Wheal was going. I was pleasantly surprised when he landed on the work of the Jesuit Paleontologist, Teilhard de Chardin. Wheal seeks a synthesis which he calls "Meaning 3.0." Teilhard was a scientist but also a Christian—a Jesuit priest. Inspired by Teilhard's vision, Wheal says it would be a mistake to scrap Christianity entirely. He says, "The Jesus meme has been virally replicating for 2,000 years." Wheal says we are wired for courage, able to grow and become Christ-like, appreciate wonder, grace and joy and make our way in hope to what Teilhard called the "Omega point."

Meaning 3.0 strikes me as a synthesis of transcendence and immanence, reason and faith, the personal and the social, a respect for science yet an awareness that reality is apprehended at a deeper level than it is comprehended. Faith is not believing without proof; it is trusting without reservation.

I like to think we at St. Paul's are a 3.0 congregation. We try to see "the other hand." We respect science. We seek to wed personal piety with social responsibility, and the best hymnody and liturgy of the past 2,000 years with sermons as current as the morning paper. We refuse to shy away from ambiguity. We believe with Teilhard that life is a journey and both heaven and the future are waiting to see what we do next.

THE RIGHT WORDS

In his poem, "Four Quartets," T.S. Eliot wrote: "words strain, crack, and sometimes break, under the burden, under the tension, slip, slide, perish, decay with imprecision, will not stay in place, will not stay still."

Poets, novelists, journalists, preachers all who make a living crafting words-know what he meant. We never know if we have used the right word or what message the word will carry. I say, "blue, blue, blue." You hear "red, red, red." I mean "yellow, yellow, yellow." Mark Twain understood when he quipped: "The difference between the right word and the nearly right word is the difference between lightning and a lightning bug." Or here is the Irish poet, Yeats: "A line will take us hours maybe. Yet if it does not seem a moment's thought, our stitching and unstitching has been naught. "

I see a youngster on the train to Philadelphia. He tells me he is going to temple. If he is wearing a yarmulke on a Friday evening, I assume he is going to a house of worship. If he is a student, carrying books, I assume he is going to the university. Words are like children. They are always in motion. When St. Paul's Cathedral in London was rebuilt after a terrible fire in 1675, Sir Christopher Wren gave Queen Anne an extensive tour. In typical British terseness, she used three adjectives to sum up her feelings: "It is awful, it is artificial, it is amusing." Sir Christopher Wren fell to his knees in gratitude. Why? You see, in 1710 the word awful meant awe-inspiring. Artificial meant artistic and amusing meant amazing!

Last week I received a note from a former member living on the west coast. She and her family were watching our Ascension Day service. A few days later her eight-year-old son was fielding fastballs from his dad in the back yard. One ball was way too fast for him "resulting in much blood, many tears and a crooked nose." A short time later, his face thoroughly iced, the boy said to his mother: "It's okay, Mom. I can handle this, no big deal. I'm bigger on the inside than I am on the outside."

The boy had taken words from a story I told about cotton candy and creatively adapted the words to his painful experience of getting hit in the face by a fast ball. I'm so glad his mom took the time to share this experience with me. We never know when our words will build up or tear down.

I love the passage in Isaiah when the Lord says, "My word shall not return to me empty but shall accomplish my purpose and succeed in the task for which I sent it." I believe God takes our words— broken and imprecise—and uses them in ways we cannot even imagine. Long after I'm gone and no longer laboring to come up with the right word, I like to think there will be a grown man—going through a painful experience—who will remember getting hit in the face by a fastball as a child and now as an adult will say again, "It's OK. I can handle this, no big deal. I'm bigger on the inside than I am on the outside."

CAPACIOUSNESS

It is wise to avoid big words. Churchill, a master of the King's English, called Hitler "that bad man." No need for a bigger word. What matters, of course, is using the best word be that word — big or small. My word today is capaciousness. It comes from the Latin word to take. It is defined as capable of containing a large quantity, spacious.

When we travel, we are aware of the capacity of our luggage. In a world where nothing stands still and today's news wraps tomorrow's fish, it is important we be capacious in our thinking. The journalist Henry Mencken once quipped that for every complex problem there is an answer that is clear, simple and wrong.

As we invite people to come back to church, we do well to heed Mencken's keen insight. If we stress rugged individualism, we risk missing the need for community. If we stress personal piety, we risk missing the need for social justice. If we stress the spirit of the day, we miss the truth of the ages.

A few times each year I meet with our newest members. I introduce them to who we are as a congregation. I remind them that each Sunday morning we will attempt to wed the best sacred music with preaching as current as the morning paper. The reason we wear traditional vestments during worship is not to draw attention to ourselves but just the opposite—to focus attention on something much bigger than ourselves. It is fitting that our choir and musicians are in the balcony. Worship is not entertainment; worship is the affirmation of God's worth. This is what Kierkegaard meant when he said: "God is the audience, we are the actors, the clergy and musicians the prompters."

Joseph Sittler taught for many years at the University of Chicago and was arguably the most creative modern Lutheran theologian. I'm sure he had "capaciousness" in mind when he wrote: "Is the opulence of the grace of God to be measured by my inventory? Is the great Catholic faith of 19 centuries to be reduced to my interior dimensions? Does the great reality of the heart of God speak only in the broken accents that I can follow after? No, that ought not to be."

A Scottish theologian once said darkness covered the earth from the sixth to the ninth hour when Jesus was crucified so no one could go home and say they saw it all. I know it's a big word, capaciousness. I've been thinking of a shorter word that does a better job. If you think of one, please let me know!

MASKS

To mask or not to mask? It's not surprising such a question—paraphrasing *Hamlet*—is apropos for t-shirts today. Shakespeare made much of masks. Disguise is one of the Bard's favorite ploys. He veils a character's identity to develop a theme, enhance the comic ambiguity or make the plot advance.

We all wear masks. Our clothing is a mask. Obscenity has been defined as exposing what should be shrouded in mystery. To know and be known is risky business. It takes courage. The 17th century poet, John Dryden spoke the truth when he said, "boldness is a mask for fear, however great." Many years ago, I titled a sermon, "The Need for Unilateral Disarmament." It was during the Vietnam War, and back there in New Jersey we had several generals in the congregation. Many in attendance no doubt thought I was going to say something controversial about our nation's involvement in that conflict. Not so. My message was all about taking the risk of being open and vulnerable in our relationships.

My grandparents often referred to their friends as Mr. or Mrs. until the relationship developed to a degree where more intimacy was in order. I understand in German "Sie" is more formal than "du." It's exciting when a relationship goes deep, and trust develops. Acquaintances become friends. So too the possibility of being hurt.

In recent weeks mask has become a fighting word. On his most recent show, Michael Smerconish interviewed two experts in pediatric medicine: one from Tufts and one from Duke. They had just written essays–one in *The New York Times* and one in *The Wall Street Journal*. One made a case for children wearing masks in school and one made a case against wearing masks in school.

In fashioning a response, I'm reminded of Paul's words: "I have become all things to all people." Paul is not inviting us to be duplicitous, disingenuously reflecting the mood of the moment. Rather he is making a case—not for capitulation but for accommodation.

The other day I was at our local library and was given a mask to wear. The rules had changed. I smiled, apologized and quickly agreed to don what was expected of me. The same expectation existed in a doctor's waiting room, and an airport terminal.

I feel strongly that our best medical science favors vaccination. I'm not so sure about the mask debate but refusing to wear a mask strikes me as arrogant and unkind. It was George Bernard Shaw who said, "The smoker and non-smoker cannot be equally free in the same railway car." My behavior always impacts my neighbor and sometimes loving my neighbor means valuing my neighbor's desires above my own. In another famous quote from St Paul: "Love is not arrogant or rude. It does not insist on its own way."

THE MANTIS AND THE LOON

Last week driving home from the Poconos I noticed a praying mantis hanging on for dear life to the outside mirror of our car. There was no way I could pull off the highway even if I so desired. I watched the poor creature for many miles wondering how long she would be able to stay with me.

I confess a sad feeling came over me when the challenge was too much for the mantis. She could hang on no longer. I thought of Zaki Anwari, 17-year-old soccer player hanging on to that plane leaving Kabul. I thought of the randomness and unpredictability of life. I thought of Charles Darwin and how he too struggled with the cruelty, waste, and suffering that accompany natural selection and evolutionary biology.

I was also keenly aware that I was observing this drama not as a biologist but as a preacher. My thoughts turned to providence. What is the meaning of all this randomness and waste? It's been going on for almost four billion years. How can I make sense of it all? Here are a few thoughts I find comforting.

First, we live in an unfinished universe. An incomplete cosmos is by definition one that has not yet been brought to perfection. If 30 volumes were to be written about the last few billion years, we humans would appear on the last few sentences of the last volume. As St. Paul wrote: "the whole creation groans in travail." God is working still, and we are called to be co-creators with God in a world still evolving.

Second, without novelty and contrast there would be only bland order. Beauty is difficult to define but implies contrast. What would day be without night, light without dark, good without evil?

Most comforting, I believe God is with us in the struggle and God's power in this world is essentially persuasive. As the French mystic, Simone Weil, put it: "God ceases to be everything so we can be something." This means we humans often derail God's plans. We are not puppets. Love is self-restricting when it comes to power. I believe there is in God's providence always a "call forward"—God is the "One who calls." We are not yet what we are meant to be. God is not finished with us.

The poet, Mary Oliver, titled one of her poems, "Lead." A loon, speckled and iridescent with a plan to fly home to some hidden lake, is dead on the shore. Why does Mary Oliver share with us this heartbreaking story?

I tell you this
to break your heart,
By which I mean only
that it break open and never close again
to the rest of the world.

This is gospel talk. The cross remains front and center. The true body is a body broken. To be is to be vulnerable. Again Simone Weil: "Frailty alone is human; a broken, a ground-up (contrite) heart."

WOKENESS

Worn-out shoes are an unusual subject choice for a painting. Yet in 1886 Vincent Van Gogh did just that. His painting of peasant shoes, housed in an Amsterdam museum, are now famous. The painting attracted the attention of one of the world's great philosophers, Martin Heidegger, who wrote a now classic work about these shoes.

It's no secret that even philosophy majors struggle to understand Heidegger. He has influenced some of the great minds of the past century, theologian Paul Tillich among them. How shocking when recently I discovered Heidegger belonged to the Nazi party and held anti-Semitic views. This was not some youthful foolishness soon outgrown. Many scholars feel this prejudice remained deep in Heidegger's psyche for decadesand existed side by side with his writings—some of the most astute essays on human existence penned in the last few centuries!

Last week a friend suggested I write a blog on wokeness and judgment. By chance Michael Smerconish interviewed columnist George Will this past Saturday. Will wasted no time in attacking wokeness and the lack of critical thinking in our modern culture. We human beings are complicated creatures. We are a mix of grime and glory, horns and haloes. In Luther's phrase, we are simul justus et peccator—saints and sinners both.

Go through history and it will be hard to find a human being who is all glory and no grime, all halo and no horn, all saint and no sinner. This is the foolishness of "political correctness" gone amuck. We can tear down statues. We can rename buildings, streets and endowed university chairs, but our demand for purity is almost always selective and myopic. Yes, fight for justice, vote for change, challenge racism but do so aware that all human motives are tainted with self-interest.

Knowing tribalism—whatever form it takes-is always the devil's ploy, invite to our campuses and churches those who don't toe the party line. Let honest debate flourish! Mix it up. Read the *Wall Street Journal* AND the *New York Times*. Don't expect teachers, columnists and preachers to affirm your views; expect them to challenge your views. As the poet Blake put it: "Without Contraries there is no progress."

I deeply regret Heidegger was such a flawed human being, but this ought not exclude him from any curriculum. Nor should we burn or ban his books. In this world ambiguity reigns. As G.K. Chesterton put it: "If I were drowning, I'd rather an atheist came by who could swim rather than a bishop who couldn't."

We humans have notions of the absolute, but we have no absolute notions. So, let us heed Jesus' words and let the wheat and weeds grow together!

PERSEVERANCE

Clemson, Kansas City Chiefs, Eagles—what happened? I think the best answer can be given in three words: nothing stays won. You are only as good as your last win. St Paul understood when he wrote to the Galatians: "You were running well, what hindered you?"

Shortly before he died last year of pancreatic cancer, Olympic champion Charlie Moore told me at lunch that he still had not gotten over being passed by Jamaican star Herb McKenley in the 4x400 relay at the '52 Helsinki Olympics. Charlie had won the gold medal in the 400-meter hurdles hours before this race, but McKenley ran an unbelievable 44.6 third leg thus nipping Charlie at the handoff to the anchor legs. The two anchors ran neck and neck, but Jamaica won the race by a yard. It was 49 years ago but for Charlie it was as fresh as the day it happened! (You can see this race on YouTube.)

Nothing stays won! This is why perseverance is such a virtue. I think of a sharp elderly lady taking a tour of Westminster Abbey. The guide waxed eloquent on the beauty and charm of this historic place of worship. The feisty old lady was not impressed and quipped: "Has anyone been saved here lately?"

I've had people not attached to the church call to schedule a baptism. They tell me how active their parents or grandparents were in the church. They may even recall a distant relative who was a pastor or missionary in a faraway place. I am always tempted to remind them that God has no grandchildren--only sons and daughters—and that the church is only one generation away from extinction. Nothing stays won!

Alan Guelzo taught history at Gettysburg College for many years and now teaches at Princeton. He just wrote a new biography of Robert E. Lee. Lee was second in his class at West Point and brilliant in many ways. Yet Lee went on to commit treason and thousands of young men lost their lives because Lee lacked the moral fiber to put nation above parochial loyalties.

Nothing stays won, but the good news of the gospel is that nothing need stay lost. Redemption is possible. What matters most is not where you've been but where you are going. God–the great alchemist—is waiting at some Damascus Road ready and eager to make our future better than our past.

The prophet Isaiah says those who wait on the Lord shall renew their strength, mount up with wings like eagles, run and not be weary, walk and not faint. It seems he got things backward. We start walking and only learn to run and fly later in life. Ah, but maybe Isaiah was suggesting a deeper truth. Maybe what takes the most courage is simply putting one foot in front of the other—after falling, getting up and keeping on keeping on!

THE END

The other day a parishioner asked me to write a blog for the elderly—those who are not thinking of the journey but the end. There comes a point in life when we are not out to break records. We know we are not as strong and agile as we once were, but we're not ready to call it quits. What then?

Erik Erikson, the famed psychologist, explored this theme deeply and came up with eight stages of human development. The last stage he called integrity vs. despair. Last week Arthur Brooks, the Harvard economist, wrote an article in *The Atlantic* in which he argues that our jobs ought not define us. He wrote that just as we often objectify others and use them for our own purposes, so too we self-objectify. One thinks of the grocer whose tombstone reads: "Born a man, died a grocer." Or the physician who was asked on the golf course by a friend: "George, what are you when you are not an M.D." George replied, "Why, I'm always an M.D."

Professor Brooks says it's not healthy for our jobs to define us. He says your profession is not your personality. His students tell him they'd rather be special than happy. Brooks tells them to have friends outside their professional circles. A great idea for sure: friends who won't drop you if you fail, who don't want your job, house, spouse, car or dog!

Brooks is not alone. Recently, social scientists have written much of how workism makes us miserable. We sacrifice love and fun for a day of work always wondering if we are successful yet. Sometimes we major in possessions or attire to show we have "made it." In *King Lear*, Shakespeare said of Edmund: "A tailor made thee." What an indictment! Brooks speaks of "sabbath-keeping." If God rested one day a week in the Genesis narrative, maybe we should too.

This is all good advice, but the gospel of Jesus Christ is not good advice but good news. Those Harvard undergraduates told Brooks they'd rather be special than happy. Frankly, I don't think his well-meaning advice will do the trick! They can do everything he says and still not feel special. What's missing, I believe, is a word from Beyond. Who tells them who they are? Friends, family, job are all part of the answer, to be sure. Yet something very primal is still missing. Vitality for most human beings requires a sense of meaning.

I believe our end is not just that we come to an end, anymore than it is the end for which a violin is made. The end for which it is made is that it should play sweet music! The old Heidelberg catechism understood. Here is the first question: "What is the chief end of man?" Answer: "The chief end of man is to glorify God and enjoy him forever."

These words were written in 1563. Try as I may, I cannot improve on them!

MEDIOCRITY

The other day a member suggested I write a blog on mediocrity. She commented that people often say, "It's good enough. During Covid we will just try to keep afloat and not expect too much." By chance, only this morning one of our college students called home to report a flat tire. A young man from the local service station not only failed to inflate the tire but caused the tire to go totally flat. He threw up his hands in despair not knowing what to do! We all have our own stories of not being ministered to by competence. What shall we make of this trend?

Is it OK to settle for mediocrity? I like this definition: mediocrity is the best of the worst and worst of the best. Only mediocrity can be trusted to be always at its best. I just read an article on grammar in which the writer said we ought not have a meltdown when we hear people say, "between you and I." I cringed. I can still see my high school English teacher diagramming sentences and reminding us to recognize and use correctly the object of a preposition. Gerunds too need to be respected!

I agree. A few quotes rush to mind that bear repeating. Mark Twain quipped that the difference between the right word and the nearly right word is the difference between lightning and a lightning bug! When we fail to grasp this truth, we end up aiming at nothing and hitting its bull's eye. It was John Gardner—Stanford scholar and swimming champion--who wrote unless our plumbers and philosophers are committed to excellence neither our pipes nor our ideas will hold any water.

How good do we have to be? In his novel, *East of Eden*, John Steinbeck tells of a boy who is rejected by his father. The message the boy gets is that he's not good enough and this rejection will color the rest of his life. In a painful memoir, novelist Pat Conroy shares a similar experience in his own life. He played basketball but his dad never felt he was good enough.

Rabbi Kushner wrote there is a difference between guilt and shame. Guilt is feeling bad for what you have done or not done; shame is feeling bad for who you are. The distinction is crucial. We can atone for the things we have done more easily than we can change who we are.

This past Sunday we celebrated Reformation Sunday, marking Luther's nailing his 95 theses on the door of the Wittenberg Church in Germany 504 years ago. It's a day we elevate in word and music the primacy of grace. Our mission statement reads: "Our worth is a divine gift not a human achievement. We have value because we are loved; we are not loved because we have value. We are not accepted by God because we are perfectly acceptable; we are accepted by God because we are perfectly loved." We are not saved by good works, but we are saved for good works.

A *New Yorker* cartoon adds this twist. A father says to his prodigal son: "Son this is the third fatted calf we've killed for you. When are you going to settle down?" Fair enough! There are fields to be mowed, cows to be milked, work to be done.

In the words of a great hymn, "Come, labor on—no time for rest till glows the western sky." Strive for excellence. Spurn mediocrity. Yet please do so not to earn your salvation or win a gold star. Do so in response to grace, in response to a love so amazing and so divine that it demands your life, your soul, your all.

TRANSCENDENCE

Yesterday a visitor greeted me after church with this observation: "I noticed a lot of Anglican elements in the service today." He seemed to enjoy our service but noted it was more formal than what he had experienced in other congregations.

I responded our aim is to combine the best of sacred music with preaching as timely as the morning paper. If I had more time, I would have shared with him my conviction that there is far more at stake here than the taste of one longtime pastor!

We pray each week "hallowed be thy name" but sadly in many churches today the forms of worship are blatantly stripped of the transcendent. One preacher put it this way: "There is music written only for the church that has no counterpart outside: the corrugated roll of a chorale, the clean line of a plainsong. How they separate us from the casual and the extraneous."

This is why your pastors and musicians avoid in worship the saccharine sentimentalism, the eroticism of the streets. God is our Lord not our pal. In his Christmas oratorio, the poet W.H. Auden has a prayer supposedly composed by Herod, who says: "I asked for a God who should be as like me as possible. What use to me is a God whose divinity consists in doing difficult things I cannot understand? There must be nothing in the least extraordinary about him."

Ah, but our God is extraordinary! The ancient Hebrews held Yahweh in such awful reverence they wouldn't write or speak the name of God. Hence in our worship we strive for reverence. We avoid the dance hall tempos, the chewing gum rhythms with the tutti frutti flavors.

So too with architecture. Many modern churches remind me of glorified Pizza Huts. I am glad I shared with my predecessor, Wilson Hartzell, my appreciation for our worship space. Before he died I wrote in an annual report: "Our nave is a magnificent space, its size a tantalizing balance between the vaultedness of a cathedral and the intimacy of a country barn. It is less ornate than many churches but hardly austere.

There is a crisp, tensile feeling to the interior, which glows with—if this makes any sense—a kind of glorious enriching restraint."

It is in the nature of chic things to come and go. Dean Inge was right: "He who marries the spirit of the age soon becomes a widower." If you think my concerns are overblown, the nostalgic longing of one more septuagenarian, I urge you to check out a recent article in the *Wall Street Journal* on the renovation of the Notre Dame Cathedral in Paris. There is a move to modernize the interior of the cathedral turning it into a theme park. The article concludes: "What a fate for the ravaged cathedral! Is that lovely victim, saved in the nick of time and whole again, now to be whisked, still groggy, straight from the hospital into the tattoo parlor of contemporary art?"

Hallowed be thy name. Yes indeed, for there is nothing like thee, O Lord, in earth or sky or sea!

PURPLE

There is a newly painted purple building at 65 W. State Street in Doylestown. I learned that TV commentator and Doylestown native Michael Smerconish bought the building and asked that it be painted a shade of purple. He said purple is a combination of red and blue and that's what he aims to be. No easy task in life or in art. Color experts tell us that one must combine shades of red and blue that work lest you end with a shade of purple sure to offend everyone!

I suggest one goal for us individuals and as a congregation in this New Year is to be a purple people. A formidable goal when Reds and Blues are shouting zealously often generating more heat than light. Back in the 1950s when Joe McCarthy and his followers saw a communist under every bed, the Yale theologian H. Richard Niebuhr wrote: "There is no greater barrier to understanding than assumption that the standpoint which we happen to occupy is a universal one." I believe it was his equally astute brother, Reinhold, who said: "We humans had notions of the absolute, but we have no absolute notions."

The evolutionary biologist E. O. Wilson died last week. He said he was no atheist, but felt most religions are tribal believing they alone are divinely favored. Perhaps if he had--in his younger years--been part of a purple church, he would have felt differently. We humans don't like to be shaken up. Ask Alice Walker, whose Pulitzer Prize winning novel, *The Color Purple*, has been banned on and off for decades!

In 2022 I hope we will continue to embrace opposites. Sandburg said of Lincoln: "He was steel in velvet." Blake: "Without contraries there is no progression." F. Scott Fitzgerald: "The test of a first-rate intelligence is the ability to hold two opposing ideas in mind at the same time and still retain the ability to function." Hegel: "No man is great unless he has in his character antitheses strongly marked." Jesus: "Be wise as serpents and innocent as doves."

Pastor Galvin, our pastor of Youth and Family Ministry, passed on to me a heavy tome by Mark Taylor, a remarkable professor at Columbia University, who attempts to combine Hegel and Kierkegaard. It was no easy read, but I warmed to his very personal confession that his dad embodied the brightness of

Hegel--reminding him the oak was always in the acorn--and his mom embodied the melancholy pensiveness of Kierkegaard.

Professor Taylor knows suffering. He is kept alive with an artificial pancreas. Teetering on the edge of death, kept alive by machines in the ICU, a nurse said to him: "I want you to know I have been praying for you." Taylor, always the academic, said from his bed: "Seeing what you see here every night, how can you still pray?" Taylor says, "with wisdom as insightful as it was innocent, she responded simply, 'How could I not?'" There is something in her response in each of us. Emily Dickinson said such doubt keeps faith nimble—a word meaning agile, anticipatory, God more Omega than Alpha!

Ah, the color purple surfacing again. May it do so in your life and mine and in the life of our church as we seek to cope creatively with ambiguity, enduring the darkness, striving to live in a wintry world as the first swallow of a new summer. Happy New Year!

SIMPLICITY

'Tis a gift to be simple. So goes the old Shaker folk song. True enough, but please don't confuse simple with simplistic! There is little good to be said about being simplistic. I believe it was the Supreme Court justice Oliver Wendell Holmes who said: "For the simplicity that lies this side of complexity, I would not give a fig, but for the simplicity that lies on the other side of complexity, I would give my life."

Take the word patriotism. I can warm to Rudyard Kipling reminding us that "God gives all men all earth to love, but since man's heart is small, ordains for each one spot shall prove beloved over all." I know what he means. Or take these words of Sir Walter Scott: "Breathes there the man with soul so dead/who never to himself hath said, / 'this is my own, my native land.' Whose heart hath n'er within him burn'd, /as home, his footsteps he has turn'd/from wandering on a foreign strand!"

Good stuff indeed! Ah, but then comes Samuel Johnson: "patriotism is the last refuge of a scoundrel." Or Robert Frost reminding us that our relationship with our native land is at best "a lover's quarrel."

Who gets it right—Kipling and Scott or Johnson and Frost? I believe the correct answer is "all of the above." This is the simplicity that lies on the far side of complexity. Simplicity is often elusive. Hence Whitehead's dictum: "Seek simplicity and distrust it." When I see a bumper sticker reading: "Jesus is the answer," I want to cry out, "What's the question?" Yet my feelings are quite the opposite when I hear of the day the theologian, Karl Barth, went to Harvard. A student asked him after his lecture to sum up the Christian religion in a simple sentence. Barth replied: "Jesus loves me this I know for the Bible tells me so."

This twelve-word answer only moves me because I know Barth has read and digested the most complex philosophical writings of the past 3,000 years. He knows the questions and has spent his life agonizing over them. Thus, his simplicity is not naïve, shallow or facile.

Vaccines, masks, isolation, loneliness, depression, eating disorders all cry out for answers. Sadly, there are those who are all too eager to give simplistic answers to these pressing problems when there are no answers capacious enough to win our full allegiance.

Thus, I leave you with a wonderful quote from the historian, Herbert Butterfield: "There are times when we can never meet the future with sufficient elasticity of mind, especially if we are locked in the contemporary systems of thought. We can do worse than remember a principle which both gives us a firm Rock and leaves us the maximum elasticity for our minds: the principle: Hold to Christ, and for the rest be totally uncommitted."

TENDERNESS

James Martin is a Jesuit priest who wrote recently about people gloating over anti-vaxxers who die of Covid. It's a sobering essay. During a recent burial, a family member turned to me and said, "People are complicated." Those three words carry much freight. The German word *schadenfreude* means taking delight in the misfortune of others. In Evelyn Waugh's *Brideshead Revisited*, a dotty father is hosting a dinner party and mentions someone whose business has failed. Another guest chuckles. Charles' father retorts: "You find his misfortune the subject of mirth?"

Yes, some anger and gloating is understandable. Columnist Tom Friedman wrote recently about Joe Rogan. On one hand, it's a good thing to have someone puncture our dogmas and question our assumptions. It would be wrong to silence those who challenge us. On the other hand, Friedman reminds us of hundreds of nurses and medical personnel who are at the breaking point, in no small part the result of false narratives Rogan has been passing on to millions.

It is to Rogan's credit that he has apologized and promised to be more careful in the future. However, no apology can undo the damage done to the anti-vaxxers who end up on ventilators--not to mention the strain put on those who are called to care for them. To those who cry out for personal freedom, I would share Bernard Shaw's words that "the smoker and non-smoker cannot be equally free in the same railway car." Freedom is not just about us. Freedom is not the right to do as we please; it is the opportunity of pleasing to do what is right!

Is our anger and indignation understandable? Yes, but schadenfreude is still a dead end. It is surely the opposite of a biblical understanding of compassion. When Jesus calls us to "love our enemies," he does not mean liking them. Loving is something you do. It is more in the will than the emotions, more a matter of courage than sentiment. The Good Samaritan had no reason to like the poor soul in the ditch, but he cares for him nonetheless.

300 years ago Samuel Johnson was right when he wrote: "kindness is in our power; fondness is not." Recently I read sad news of someone who apparently made some bad decisions. I was shocked at the

cruelty of many who responded. I wish I could remind them there is no freedom in withheld compassion. As Eldridge Cleaver put it: "The price of hating another is loving yourself less."

People are complicated! One day we too may need compassion. We cannot live without pity. Empathy means not just feeling for the afflicted but feeling with them. It is one of life's great paradoxes that it's in the crucible of pain and suffering that we become tender.

MISSING THE MISSISSIPPI

A few weeks ago, knowing I'd be flying home from Florida, I spotted a paperback in a used bookstore. It was Mark Twain's *Life on the Mississippi*. On sale for a dollar, it was a bargain I could not resist—a good read for the two-hour flight home. Mark Twain was bewitched by the river. He drank it in with speechless rapture. There is nothing to equal the childlike wonder of seeing something for the first time.

Mark Twain, not one given to foolish sentiment, reflects on whether he has gained most or lost most by learning his trade. As a river pilot, it is his calling to master the language of this water, to know every trifling feature of the river, but he lost something too. All the grace, the beauty, the poetry had gone out of the majestic river. In time he no longer notes the glories and charms which the moon and the sun and the twilight wrought upon the river's face.

As I continued reading, our pilot announced we were about to land. My mind was spinning. I thought of a lovely poem by Thomas Hood:

I remember, I remember, the fir trees dark and high
I used to think their slender tops were close against the sky:
It was a childish ignorance but now 'tis little joy,
To know I'm farther off from heav'n than when I was a boy.

Wordsworth understood too. He said, "heaven lies about us in our infancy." What happened to Mark Twain can happen to us. The years go by more quickly as we age. We've been here before. Been there done that. G.K. Chesterton has this "appetite for infancy" in mind when he pictures a child during a thunderstorm. Face pressed against the windowpane, the child shouts: "Do it again, God, do it again."

"Where is the wisdom we have lost in knowledge?" ruminates the poet T.S. Eliot. Mensa is an organization composed of those with the highest IQs. The last I heard they were unable to agree on a simple constitution.

Jesus told us unless we became as little children, we will never enter the kingdom of God. I wonder if he had trees and rivers in mind when he made that observation?

One of our nation's most stellar theologians captured what I'm trying to share with you. Reinhold Niebuhr, after years of relating Scripture to the political machinations of his day, wrote this:

"Perhaps the difference between childishness and childlikeness is that the latter recaptures rather than retains the simplicities and profundities of childhood. The one who can see in childhood the promise of what life ought to be, and the outline of what life truly is, has discerned one of the profoundest truths of the Christian religion."

ABOUT THE AUTHOR

Robert H. Linders has served as senior pastor of St. Paul's Lutheran Church in Doylestown, Pennsylvania since August 1977. One of the largest Lutheran congregations in the greater-Philadelphia area, the church celebrated its 150th anniversary in 2011.

He was ordained in 1967 following his graduation with a master of divinity degree from The Lutheran Theological Seminary at Philadelphia. A graduate of Gettysburg College, he also holds an M.A. in English from Monmouth College in New Jersey. In addition, he has earned master's and doctoral degrees, both from Princeton Theological Seminary.

The New Jersey State Champion in the 800 meter run in 1960, he was the Most Valuable Athlete in his high school graduating class at Northern Valley Regional High School in Demarest. He was inducted into the inaugural Hall of Fame class at his high school in 2011. In 1964 he represented the United States in a dual track meet against Great Britain in London, England. He was inducted into the College Hall of Athletic Honor at Gettysburg College in 2001. His 800 meter record of 1:50.7 has been unsurpassed at Gettysburg for 58 years.

He has lectured or preached at Catholic, Princeton, Cornell and Penn State Universities, as well as The Lutheran Theological Seminary at Philadelphia. In addition, he has conducted numerous seminars on preaching.

His publications include "Preaching About Evil," an article in Homiletical Accents; sermons in the book Selected Sermons published by the Episcopal Church; articles in Partners and Theology Today; as well as an article included in Book of Readings used in the Second International Ecumenical Congress on the Meaning of Human Suffering in Houston, Texas. He has also published two books of sermons and essays: *No Time for Rest*, and *No Safe Route*.

He has inspired eight members of St. Paul's to enter the seminary and prepare for the ordained ministry.

From 1970 to 1977, he served as pastor of Lutheran Church of the Reformation, West Long Branch, New Jersey. From 1967 to 1970, he was pastor of Holy Trinity Lutheran Church, Leonia, New Jersey.